Interviews From the Bible

The stories of Jesus told by
those who knew him first

Doug Hallman

authorHOUSE®

AuthorHouse™
1663 Liberty Drive
Bloomington, IN 47403
www.authorhouse.com
Phone: 833-262-8899

Published by AuthorHouse   02/25/2022

ISBN: 978-1-6655-5252-3 (sc)
ISBN: 978-1-6655-5263-9 (e)

Library of Congress Control Number: 2022903418

Print information available on the last page.

Contents

Acknowledgments vii
Preface ix

1. **Joseph,** father of Jesus 1
   Matthew 1:18-24

2. **John,** Jesus' cousin 14
   Matthew 3:1-4

3. **Peter,** the fisherman..27
   Matthew 4:18-22, Luke 5:1-11

4. **A Blind Man** healed 40
   Mark 8:22-26

5. **A Samaritan Woman** at the well 52
   John 4:1-42

6. **Philip,** the Evangelist... 64
   John 14:8-11

7. **John Mark,** an eyewitness....................................79
   Mark 14:51, Acts 12:25

8. **Thomas,** the twin 94
   John 11:11-16

9. **Nicodemus,** a Pharisee 107
    John 3:1-18

10. **Pontius Pilate,** the governor 123
    Luke 23:1-25

11. **Mary Magdalene,** first to the tomb 137
    Luke 8:1-3

12. **James,** brother of Jesus 153
    Acts 15:13-21; 21:18

13. **Luke,** the doctor 167
    Colossians 4:14

14. **Peter,** the rock 184
    John 21, Acts 2

15. **A Boy** and his lunch 197
    John 6:1-14, Matthew 5:1 - 7:29

Acknowledgments

Many thanks to the members of the BYKOTA (Be Ye Kind One to Another) Sunday School Class for their encouragements to publish these chapters which were first presented to them as Sunday morning lessons.

Great appreciation is due to my wife, RayaSue, for her patience during the months of writing and proofreading of these pages.

Preface

Tell me the stories of Jesus I love to hear;
Things I would ask him to tell me if he were here;
Scenes by the wayside, tales by the sea,
Stories of Jesus, tell them to me.

It is highly unlikely that any of the writers of the four gospels in our Bibles ever knew Jesus. Mark was a young cousin of Barnabas who travelled with him and Paul. Luke was a companion of Paul who wasn't even from Judea. The Gospel of Matthew makes no claim for or gives any information as to its author. There is great debate over whether the writer of the Gospel of John was one of the original twelve or a later leader in the early church, perhaps one known as "the Elder John."

That being the case, all the material in the gospels must have been gathered by these writers through interviews with those who were there and witnessed the events. We know, for example, that Luke learned the stories of Jesus from his time with Paul and his one recorded visit to Jerusalem where he had the opportunity to meet "all the elders."(Acts 21:15-18)

How great would it be to be able to talk to someone who knew Jesus? To have someone who was there tell us what Jesus was like? What was Jesus like as an older brother or a cousin? What happened to those he healed after he healed them? What did his disciples think about him?

Have you ever wished that you could hear directly from some of the people who knew Jesus? What were their lives like? How did they meet Jesus? What was their impression of Jesus? What impact did their time with Jesus have on their lives? Wouldn't it be wonderful to be able to ask them questions and to hear, in their own words, how their encounters with Jesus took place? However, except for the twelve disciples and a few of their family members, we don't even know most of their names.

There are scraps of information scattered throughout the Gospels that can help us piece together a somewhat more detailed profile of at least some of those unnamed individuals. The persons "interviewed" in this book all knew (some more intimately than others), or at least encountered Jesus.

The stories that are told in these interviews are all drawn from evidence in the Gospels. For the back-stories, I have drawn on information from early church writers and traditions as well as secular historical sources. I have tried not to introduce any information that is not compatible with what is known from these sources. For example, because of the passages in the Book of Acts where the author uses the first-person pronoun "we", we assume that the author (Luke) travelled with Paul at some points along the way. The designation of Luke as a "physician" brings to my mind the questions, "How did Luke become a doctor? When did he become interested in medicine? Where did he gain his medical knowledge?" The fact that we first hear about Luke coming into the company of Paul in the region of Mysia, and that we know from Roman documents that Pergamum, in that same region, was home to a major medical center, leads me to think that is where he "caught the medical bug" and perhaps received his training. None of that is "biblical" but it all seems possible when you fit those scant pieces of information together.

My hope for this book is that these interviews might make these people come alive in the mind of the reader and through them come to a more intimate relationship with the Jesus who is friend and brother to all of us.

The conversations are all fiction but were written with an effort made to reflect the circumstances and personality of those who knew Jesus. I hope you enjoy "hearing" from some of the people who knew Jesus first.

Chapter 1

Joseph, father of Jesus
Matthew 1:18-24

THE FIRST INTERVIEW IN THIS book is with Joseph, son of Jacob, husband of Mary, a carpenter in Galilee.

Interviewer: Joseph, we are interested in what you can tell us about the life of Jesus. Perhaps you could begin with what you remember about events that took place on the night he was born?

Joseph: What a wild and crazy night that was! We had arrived in Bethlehem late in the afternoon. We needed to find a place to stay. We had seen thousands of travelers on the road, so I knew that it would not be an easy thing to do. Most of those travelers passed us by because we had to go so slowly due to Mary's condition. She was in her last days before giving birth, and it was hard for her to sit on that donkey for long; but it was even harder for her to walk.

Knowing that all the others were headed in the same direction, I became worried about where we would find a place. I knew that, as a last resort, I had an uncle who ran a small hostel in Bethlehem. It had been a few years since I had any contact with him so I didn't really know if he was still in business or not – or if he was even still alive! I didn't tell Mary of my worries. I just kept reassuring her that everything would work out.

Sure enough, when we arrived, there were people everywhere. Every place we stopped to inquire about a room we were turned away. After asking several people if they knew my uncle, we were given directions to his place on the edge of town.

When I knocked on the door, a young boy opened the door, and before I could say anything, he said, rather roughly, "Go away mister, we ain't got no room here for nobody else," and he slammed the door.

I had run out of options. I turned to go and told Mary that we would find a nice place under a tree somewhere and we could look at the stars all night. But before we got very far, the door of the inn opened and a man's voice said, "Young man, how can I help you?" Those were the most comforting words I had heard on that whole journey.

When I turned around, my uncle recognized me and said, "Joseph! I was hoping I might see you in town this week. Come in. And who is this with you?" "This is Mary. We are soon to be married, but she is already with child, I said, and we need a place to make her comfortable."

His face dropped as he said, "I'm so sorry, we are already sold out." "How about just a place on the floor by the fire?" I asked.

He thought for a moment and then said, "No, that would be too dangerous. That's a pretty rough crowd in there. But I have an idea. Follow me."

We walked around to the back of the building and down a short path where there was a large cave opening. Uncle was using it as a stable for his livestock. There were also chickens and goats scurrying everywhere. He led us inside to a dark corner in the back of the cave where there was a pile of fresh straw. He said, "Make yourselves as comfortable as you can here, and I will send my wife out to help Mary through the night.

It wasn't long before his wife came out and realized that Mary was just about to give birth. I was sent to gather some clean rags from the house. When I came back, I could hear the sounds of a baby crying before I even got to the cave. I gave the cloths to the innkeeper's wife and she used them to wrap the baby. He was so beautiful and peaceful looking. Mary seemed to be fine – a little worn out, but okay. We thanked my uncle's wife, and before she left, she asked us what the baby's name was going to be. Without skipping a beat, Mary and I said together, "Jesus."

Soon Mary fell asleep with Jesus cuddled on her breast. Some of the little animals were curious and crept closer and closer. I tried to keep them back, but Mary said they intended no harm, so I sat down to rest and let them come and look. I don't know how long I slept, but it didn't seem like very long before I could hear voices outside the cave. As I stood to protect Mary and Jesus, a little boy holding a very small lamb stuck his head around the corner and said, "Mister, is there a baby here? We came to see the baby."

And then several more of them stepped around the corner. It was obvious they were shepherds. Upon seeing Mary and the baby, they knelt down and began praying. All I could think of was, "Who are these people and how did they get here? How did they know about Jesus since he was only a couple hours old?"

When they finished praying, the leader stood up and told me a most unbelievable tale of things that had happened that night. He said there had been angels and bright lights and music from the heavens. They said that one angel told them that this baby, our baby, would be the savior of the world! They said he would bring peace to the world. I thought, I am just a carpenter; how can my child be expected to do anything as great as that? Then I remembered, this was not my child. Mary had told me about the angel that came to her and told her that her child would be the child of God. At first I didn't trust her, but then that same angel told me not to be afraid to take Mary for my wife because she had not been unfaithful to me, but that she had been chosen by God to be the mother of his child.

Our visitors didn't stay too long. I think they could see just how tired we were. After they left, Mary and I looked at each other and asked each other what we thought this meant. We had no idea what was about to happen next. We were soon asleep.

Interviewer: We've heard that the shepherds weren't the only visitors that night. Can you tell us about that?

Joseph: We weren't able to sleep long. Just before daylight we again heard people approaching the cave. A lot of voices speaking words I couldn't understand. When I looked up there were three very important and very rich-looking men standing there. They were foreign but I didn't recognize their clothing or the language they were speaking. They didn't look like they were there to do us harm, but I couldn't tell what they wanted. One by one they approached the manger where we had placed Jesus. Each one knelt down in a most humble manner before the manger. As they did, each one mumbled a prayer and placed some sort of fancy looking container on the ground.

After offering their gifts, they summoned a man who could translate their words for us. He told us they were from somewhere in the east that I had never heard of. They said they had been guided for a long time by a new star that had never before been charted. I don't know if they were kings or not – but they sure looked like it.

They told us that in their religion they were considered elders among the priests and that they studied the patterns of the stars, looking for messages from their gods. They said they believed that a new star in the sky would be the sign of a new king on earth, and that is why they followed it. Because that new star had led them to Bethlehem and to the cave where we were sleeping, they believed that our baby would become a great king and would lead the world in a new direction. It didn't seem to matter to them that they were honoring a baby who had been born in a cold, dark cave filled with the smells of animals.

They told us that even our own king, King Herod, expressed interest in finding the baby so he, also, could honor it and that Herod wanted them to return to him and tell him where we were. Soon they were gone, and again Mary and I were left standing there wondering what had just happened.

When we reached down and opened the boxes they had left at the foot of the manger, we couldn't believe our eyes! In one box was a purse containing more gold coins than I had ever seen before! Inside the next one was a sack holding pieces of something that smelled good. Mary had to tell me that it was frankincense which was very expensive in the markets. The third box contained a fancy decanter of myrrh oil which is often used to prepare the dead for burial, among other uses. We were dumbfounded. We had never had such expensive things before.

Remembering what those three men told us about their encounter with old King Herod, I told Mary that we both knew that King Herod was not to be trusted to do anything good. If he was looking for our baby, it wasn't so that he could offer an expensive gift! The more we thought about what those men had said that "our king wanted to find Jesus so he could honor him," the more suspicious I became. I told Mary that we had to get out of there before Herod came looking for us.

We began to form a plan of where to go while we rested in that stable for another night. The next day, while my uncle's wife stayed with Mary and the baby, I found the place where I had to register for the census and pay the tax. The morning of Jesus' third day, without telling anyone of our plan, we slipped out of Bethlehem before dawn and headed south toward Egypt. I left a note for my uncle thanking him for his kindness toward us. I wrapped the note around one of the gold coins the stranger had given me and placed it in the manger where Jesus had been sleeping.

After several days walking through the desert, we ended up in a small village in Egypt. If it hadn't been for the hospitality of several Bedouin families along the way, I doubt we would have survived. I was able to find some small jobs in Egypt to keep us going. It is a good thing that I always carried a few basic tools with me. Our days in Egypt were pleasant enough. We watched Jesus grow and learn to walk and talk. It seemed that he was speaking Egyptian as much as he was learning our own language.

Then one night when Jesus was almost two years old, I saw that angel again in my sleep. He told me that it was safe to return home since old King Herod had died. We made arrangements to leave and by then I was able to afford a slightly larger animal for Mary and Jesus to ride on that would make them a little more comfortable.

Interviewer: When you returned, there is some question in the reports we have as to whether you settled in Bethlehem or in Nazareth. Can you clarify that for us?

Joseph: Yes. We first returned to Bethlehem where I had hopes that my uncle could help me find work since we had a lot of family there and he seemed to know a lot of people. When we got there, he welcomed us into his home, but told us that it was too dangerous for us to stay in Judea because the new king Herod was continuing his father's policy of murdering children while looking for our son!

He asked around and learned that there was a lot of construction going on in Sepphoris, up in Galilee. After they loaded us with provisions and some housewares that we would need, we said our fond goodbyes and headed out on the road again. Instead of risking going through Jerusalem, we headed west toward Joppa. From there we followed the coast north to Mt. Carmel where there is a pass through the mountains inland toward Sepphoris.

As we looked around, we knew there was no way we could afford a place in that town. We quickly learned that most of the builders and masons and carpenters all lived in Nazareth, about five miles south of the town. That's how we ended up in Nazareth. Just as Uncle had said, there was an abundance of work in the area. We found a small house with a very small shed in the back that I was able to turn into a workshop where I could make furniture and spend more time at home. But in the beginning it was five miles down the hill to work and five miles up again in the evening.

Interviewer: Tell us about what Jesus was like growing up in Nazareth.

Joseph: What a great kid he was. All the neighbors loved him and all the kids wanted to play with him. It wasn't long before I was introducing myself around town as "Jesus' father," and they all knew who I was talking about.

Jesus did great in school. I only remember a couple of times when he got into some trouble. As he told me, he was just trying to break up a fight and save some little kid from getting beaten up. I told him that I was proud of him for sticking up for the little guy, but encouraged him to find another way to stop the fight before it ever got started.

Jesus always liked working in the shop with me and quickly became quite proficient using my tools. He liked to take a scrap of wood that I had tossed aside thinking it was useless and carve it until he had made something useful out of it – a lamp holder or something like that. After a while, I began to take him along on the job with me and he was a great help, not only with the job, but with the customers who could, sometimes, be quite difficult to have around. Jesus had a way of sensing when something was bothering them, and I often would glance over and see him sitting with the man or woman of the house in the shade and involved in what seemed to be a deep conversation.

On the way home when I asked him what they had been talking about, he would tell me their whole, long story – their griefs about their children, their concerns about paying all the taxes the Romans were demanding, all the illnesses in the family, and so on. When I asked him how he found out all that information, he said that he mostly just listened. He said he could see most of it in their faces and the way they stood. I don't know just what he said to them, but I could absolutely see the difference in their attitude the following day. Soon I was having people asking me to be sure and bring Jesus with me to the job site so they could continue their conversations.

When he was twelve we decided to take him with us to Jerusalem for the Passover celebration. He had been begging us to go every year.

Interviewer: And how did that go?

Joseph: What a glorious trip that turned out to be! We traveled in the company of several other family members and neighbors. The feast was eaten in the home of some distant relations including my aunt and uncle from Bethlehem. When we all left the city, I thought Mary knew where Jesus was so I didn't say anything when he didn't show up for supper. That night, Mary turned to me and asked me where Jesus was. I said, "I thought you knew." "No," she said," I figured you had given him permission to stay with his cousins or someone." We both began to panic and started searching through the whole camp, waking people up asking them if they had seen Jesus!

In the morning we turned around and returned to Jerusalem where there were still mobs of "Passover pilgrims." We searched for three days! We finally decided to go to the temple and make an offering and pray for God's protection over Jesus.

As we entered the temple courtyard, I saw a group of rabbis walking toward the sanctuary all clustered together.

There, in the middle of them was Jesus! I shouted out to him as I ran as fast as I could toward him. When I got him in my arms, I didn't know if I was more relieved or angry.

When Mary caught up to us, we asked him what he was thinking leaving us like that. We told him that we had been extremely worried about him. He apologized for causing us such worry and then said, "But I thought you would know that I would be safe here in my Father's house." One of the rabbis that Jesus had been with could see that we were angry at Jesus. He approached us to say that our Jesus was a most remarkable young man. He told us that Jesus had been asking the most insightful questions and had a deep and profound knowledge of the Law and the Prophets.

Interviewer: And how did that make you feel?

Joseph: All the way home I thought about that rabbi's words. They reminded me of what the angel had said to me when he told me to name the baby "Jesus." He said it was because he would "save his people from their sins." And I remembered the visits from those shepherds who said angels sent them, and the rich men who gave us those expensive gifts and how they said our son would grow up to be a mighty king.

I never truly understood all of those things, but I could see something in Jesus that was different from the other boys. He was always loving toward everyone. He couldn't stand to see someone hurt, and he would never stand back while an injustice was being committed without stepping in on behalf of the one being unjustly treated.

I often wondered why God chose me to be a part of Jesus' life. It was obvious why Mary was chosen. She was the most compassionate and kind person I ever knew. She never gave much thought to herself but was always thinking about and doing for others. She taught all the children to be aware of the needs of others and to look for ways to help. But me? I was just a rough old carpenter. What could I offer? But I figured that for whatever reason I was chosen, the best I could do was to do what I did best. I always tried to teach Jesus to be patient and careful – both with the material he was working with as well as the people we dealt with.

I would often tell Jesus the story of Noah and how he built the ark out of wood to the specifications that God gave him even though there was no water around and he didn't know why God wanted a boat. And how Noah and his sons kept building while all the people laughed at him for doing what God instructed. I would remind him that the ark was just a vessel to carry animals and a few people into a new world, and that there would have been no ark if there hadn't been a carpenter who knew how to build it and was willing to obey God.

My favorite verse was one from the prophets. It was one that I tried to teach to Jesus as we worked together. It is from the words of the prophet Haggai from back when our people were returned from exile and were rebuilding Jerusalem and the temple. Haggai said,

"This is what the Lord of heavenly forces says: Take your ways to heart. Go up to the highlands and bring back wood. Rebuild the temple so that I may enjoy it, and that I may be honored, says the Lord." (Haggai 1:7-8)

I would tell Jesus that the wood and stone we used in building were gifts from God, and that though we may not be building a magnificent temple where multitudes would worship, the simple houses we built were just as important to the families who would live there. And we needed to remember that the God of the ages would reside there with those families. We must always be mindful that whatever we built would be our offering to God.

I wish I had gotten to spend more years with Jesus and the family, but I hope whatever influence I had on Jesus encouraged him to be a man of compassion and truth, and one in which others could find a comforter and friend.

Interviewer: Joseph, we thank you for your time today, and I want to assure you that Jesus did grow into a man you would have been most proud of. In fact, his influence on people has truly changed the world.

Chapter 2

John, Jesus' cousin
Matthew 3:1-4

FOR THIS INTERVIEW, WE WILL be speaking with one of Jesus' relatives - John, son of the priest Zechariah and his wife Elizabeth. Zechariah and Elizabeth lived in a small village a few miles up the road from Jerusalem. The village named Ein Karem is about 4.5 miles west of Jerusalem. The town is mentioned in Jeremiah 6:1 as the location of one of a series of signal fires that provided a communications link between Jerusalem and the north to warn of any impending invasion. As with most ancient towns, it was built around a spring. The spring's name, Ein Karem, meant "spring of the vineyard." Today it is called "Mary's Spring" and is believed to be the place where Mary met Elizabeth and the baby Jesus "jumped" in Mary's womb.

Interviewer: Good morning sir. We are eager to learn what you can tell us about Jesus. To begin with, can you tell us how you and Jesus were related?

John: Of course. My mother was the sister of Jesus' grandmother, Anne. That made Jesus my cousin of some degree or another.

Interviewer: And were you and Jesus close when you were growing up?

John: We were actually close before we were born!

Interviewer: How so?

John: As soon as Jesus' mother found out she was pregnant, she came to stay with my mother and father for a while to help take care of my mother during her final months before I was born. The way my mother told it, as soon as she saw Mary coming up the walk, she felt me jump in her womb for the first time! I suppose that's when our closeness began.

Interviewer: I understand there is an interesting story about how you were given the name "John." We would love to hear you tell that story.

John: Mother and father had waited a long time to have children – in fact, they had almost given up. Once, when Dad was on duty at the temple, and the best Mother could remember, while he was alone in the Holy of Holies offering prayers, an Angel showed up and announced that a baby was on the way and they should name him "John."

Apparently, because dad questioned the possibility of two old people having a child, the Angel took away his ability to speak until I was born and given the name "John." It must have been funny watching dad trying to say all that with just his hands! When I was born, all the townspeople thought I would be named Zechariah after my father. But Mom told them it would be "John". When dad confirmed the name by writing it on a tablet, he could suddenly speak again!

The name "John" means "God is gracious" and my mother and father certainly felt that God had been gracious to them by giving them a son at their ages. When he could speak again, father told more of what the angel had told him. He said, "Your son will be great in the Lord's eyes. He must not drink wine or liquor. He will be filled with the Holy Spirit even before his birth. He will bring many Israelites back to the Lord their God. He will go forth before the Lord, equipped with the spirit and power of Elijah. He will turn the hearts of fathers back to their children, and he will turn the disobedient to righteous patterns of thinking. He will make ready a people prepared for the Lord." (Luke 1:15-17)

Well, let's see, where were we? What was your question?

Interviewer: Were you and Jesus close when you were growing up?

John: As much as possible. You see, people didn't travel as much back then as you do today. Most of the times I had the chance to spend time with Jesus were during the festivals when his family would come to Jerusalem. Sometimes they would stay with us on their way to the city.

When we did get together, we got along well. Since Jesus was a serious student of the scriptures and my father was a priest who taught at the synagogue school in our town, Jesus and I enjoyed talking about the history of our people and what the words of the prophets were saying to our generation. We would spend hours discussing what God was going to do to help the Jews in our day.

We spent a lot of time talking about the prophecies concerning the promised messiah. Who might it be? When would he appear? Where would he come from? How would we be able to identify him? How would he free us from the oppressive rule of Rome? Those sorts of things.

Interviewer: And what answers did the two of you come up with about the Messiah?

John: Well, to tell you the truth, we were of two differing opinions. Jesus was a whole lot more patient in his anticipation than I was. He kept saying, "The will of God will be done here on earth when God is ready." I was a lot more impatient and kept making the point that until people changed, there wasn't much God could do to help us.

My thought was that we had to sweep out all the angry and hateful ways we had been treating each other before we could do anything different. I told him it was like when his father was building a house – he had to clear the land of all the rubbish that was there so he could lay a solid foundation. He had to prepare the site. People needed to change their ways before they could live the way God intends. More than once Jesus told me that maybe I should be the person to tell people that!

As the years went on, we saw less and less of each other. Jesus led a quiet life up north, working as a builder and carpenter. Now and then I heard about him teaching in the synagogue and how people were truly amazed at the wisdom he imparted.

I began studies for the priesthood like my father, but the more I was around the other priests, the more disillusioned I became. I watched as they would come out of the temple and just step over some beggar lying there. I saw them push aside the blind who crossed their path. The only thing they seemed interested in was showing how important they were by the way they dressed or the way they looked down on the sick and poor. They couldn't be bothered with the problems of people in pain or distress. You see, they had all memorized the laws and teachings of the prophets, but most of them had no idea what those laws were all about. The idea that they should help people who suffered never came to their minds!

They prided themselves on keeping every little commandment, especially when it came to how to worship God in the temple. They knew which animal to sacrifice for which sins. They knew how many steps you were allowed to take on the Sabbath and what constituted work that you were supposed to avoid. They knew what foods could be eaten with what other foods, who you could be seen talking with, and who you had to avoid. As they walked around, you could just see how proud they were thinking that they were pleasing God by keeping all of those picky little laws, but doing nothing to really help anyone.

What you couldn't see, at least I couldn't, was any intention of going out of their way to help those in need – especially if it meant breaking or cracking a law just a little. They had convinced themselves that anybody who was not as obviously "holy" as they were was obviously an irreligious sinner who deserved to be ostracized. And if the crippled or anyone with signs of leprosy got in their way, well, forget it.

I tried to talk about what our job as priests really was meant to be, but I was told to fall in line and just do what the High Priest told me to do.

The time came when I couldn't live with myself any longer if that was the attitude I was supposed to have. I walked away. I just left. I knew about a group out in the desert who were trying to live differently, so I joined them. But I soon felt confined by their strict interpretations of the law. I left there and had been living on my own in the desert when I remembered Jesus saying that I could be the one to tell the people that God was going to send the Messiah.

My excuse had always been that I was awkward when speaking to people. I was no scholar like Jesus. Out there, alone in the wilderness, I prayed for God to give me a purpose, something that I could do. I kept thinking about Isaiah's prophesy, "A voice will cry out in the wilderness saying 'Clear a path for the Lord; make a level highway; clear away the rubble; straighten out the road.'" Eventually, God told me that I could be that voice! So I decided to give it a try.

I went to a spot along the river close to Jerusalem where there was a crossing and people were always coming and going. I waded out a little way into the water and began to shout to the crowds. "The Lord is coming!" I shouted, "and you must change your ways. You must repent of your wickedness and greed. You must wash your hearts and be made clean for the coming of the Lord." At first people just stared at me and kept going, but soon they were stopping and listening. Some even came down into the water and began to lift the water over their heads in a sign of repentance as they prayed.

It was a simple act of contrition and it seemed to make a difference in those people – at least for a while. But there were those who took a much dimmer view of what was happening. They asked me, "Who are you? Are you the Messiah?" I was astounded that they would come to that conclusion since I had said nothing to give that impression. "No, absolutely not. I am not the Messiah," I replied. "Then who are you?" they demanded. "I am just that one crying in the wilderness for the people to prepare a straight path to their hearts to welcome the Lord who is coming soon, just as the prophet Isaiah said."

"Then why do you baptize these people if you aren't the Messiah?" they argued. "I baptize with water as a sign of the washing away of sins -- that's all. But there is one coming after me who will baptize the people with God's very own Spirit. I am not even worthy to untie the straps of his sandals."

The very next day I saw him standing in the back of the crowd.

Interviewer: Who?

John: My cousin, Jesus.

I waved for him to come forward so he could help me. I told those who had been questioning me, "This is the one I was telling you about. The one who is much greater than I am." When he reached me, I knelt down in the river for him to baptize me. But he told me to get up and to baptize him so that God's righteousness could be fulfilled. I wasn't sure I knew what he meant, but I poured the water over his head. He was looking up and praying.

Suddenly he said, "Look John! Do you see it?" "See what?" I said. Then I, too, looked up and saw a bright light and what appeared to be a bird, maybe a dove descending from the heavens and lighting on Jesus' shoulder. And I heard a voice that said, "This is my beloved son." I swear it was the voice of God! I said to Jesus, "Yes, Lord, I see it and I hear it." When Jesus stood up he gave me the mightiest hug I had ever received and he said, "Keep doing what you are doing John. God needs the world to hear your message. Now I must go and get ready." I watched as he left and I knew that the time had come for God's will to be done here on earth as it always has been done in heaven. I knew God was ready!

I continued my ministry of calling people to repent and prepare for God to come to them. I moved up and down the river until one day, when I was up in the region of Galilee, I heard the people mumbling about the Herod who was ruling that district.

This was Herod Antipas, son of Herod the Terrible and his wife, Malthace. Antipas met and proposed marriage to his niece, Herodias. Herodias was the granddaughter of Herod the Terrible and was married to Antipas' half-brother, and her own uncle, Philip. They had a daughter, Salome.

Herodias agreed to leave Philip and marry another uncle, Antipas. All of this was very immoral and went against the Torah law. Shortly after I called him out on it, I was arrested. They literally pulled me out of the river and dragged me off to prison. I later learned that Herodias had put pressure on Antipas to silence me for making her look bad, and that actually Antipas was somewhat afraid of me since he thought of me as a "holy man."

No prison is comfortable, but it was obvious that I wasn't being held in the worst part of Herod's jail, probably because of his secret admiration of me and his frequent habit of visiting me. He had endless questions about faith and the warnings of the prophets. I could tell that he was a troubled man. He knew that his relationship with Herodias was wrong. I sensed that he was looking for a way out of it. He was struggling.

While I was in prison those many months, my friends were given permission to visit me and bring provisions. They reported to me on what Jesus was doing. On one occasion, I instructed some of my men to go to Jesus and ask him directly if he was the Messiah or were we still to wait for another. What they reported to me reassured my spirit. They told me that when they arrived, Jesus was very busy, so they stood back and just watched how he dealt with those who crowded around him.

They saw him cure many people of all manner of diseases. They saw him cast out evil spirits. They watched as he brought sight to those who were blind. They saw those who were feverish and having difficulty even breathing suddenly become calm and able to take deep breaths. Crutches were thrown aside and lepers were made clean. They told me that it didn't matter who they were, Jesus would take time with them--talk with them, pray with them, and rejoice with them in their healing. He told my disciples to return to me and tell about the things they had seen.

As they were leaving Jesus, they told me that they could hear Jesus telling the crowd that I was the one God sent to prepare the way before his Son. They said Jesus told them that "among those born of women," no one was greater than me. That was high praise coming from my own cousin.

Interviewer: John, what would your message be for the world today?

John: Well, in some aspects, I don't think your day is that much different from my day. People don't really change much from one generation to the next. And the big problem people of all ages face is fear. Fear that throws dark shadows over life and prevents people from experiencing complete joy.

Interviewer: What kind of fears are you referring to?

John: Most people are not so much afraid of the things that happen to them as they are of the things that are within them. They know it is wrong, but they covet things they are not entitled to. And because they know they do that, they are afraid that someone else will try to take what is theirs. People are afraid of the anger that stirs within them because they know how destructive it is. They are afraid of the hatred they feel towards others because hatred only ends up in conflict with hatred, and there are no winners in that fight.

People know that God watches over us and they are afraid that God will not like what he sees when he looks at us. Coveting what is not yours, holding on to anger and hatred toward others -- these are the things that create darkness. These are the curtains that darken the house of the soul. That block out the light. People who walk in such darkness avoid the light because they know what they do is wrong. So they stumble around and fall and live in fear of God's judgment.

But people need to hear that there is a great light that shatters the darkness and reveals joy to all the world. Jesus said that light is the love that the Father holds for the whole world. He once told me that the light of God's love is so strong and powerful that darkness will never be able to put it out.

People are so afraid of what they have done that they are afraid of what God will do to them. But the truth is that God loves everyone in the world. God loves us so much that he sent his own Son into the world to show that love to us.

Interviewer: What would be your advice to the church today?

John: Don't stop telling the world about God's unending love. That has always been the greatest news people who continue to struggle along in darkness long to hear. Tell them with your words. Tell them by loving them. Tell them by how you treat them. Tell them by welcoming them. Don't judge them. Don't condemn them. Don't be afraid of them. Show them love.

In my day I was looked on as a little strange. I didn't dress like others. I lived in the wilderness and confess to have eaten a grasshopper or two when I could find nothing else. I wasn't a trained public speaker and didn't have any credentials to validate my ministry. But God called me, and eventually I responded and did the best I could.

I hope those who know Jesus in your day will speak up and tell the world about the light that has brought joy and peace into their lives. People can change from the ways that lead to darkness and follow the light that leads to eternal life.

If I may, let me share with you from the words of the prophet Isaiah that always gave me hope.

Interviewer: Please do.

John: To the people of Israel living in the darkness of exile, the prophet said, "Arise! Shine! Your light has come;

the Lord's glory has shone upon you. Though darkness covers the earth and gloom the nations, the Lord will shine upon you; God's glory will appear over you. The Lord will be your everlasting light; your God will be your glory." (Isaiah 60)

Interviewer: Thank you so much John for your time and for your timeless witness.

Chapter 3

Peter, the fisherman
Matthew 4:18-22, Luke 5:1-11

THIS INTERVIEW IS WITH THE disciple known as "The Big Fisherman" or "The Rock," as Jesus called him. His given name was Simon. Later he became the first bishop of Rome.

Interviewer: Peter, we are honored to have you with us today. Could you please tell us how you met Jesus and what your relationship was like with him in the beginning?

Peter: It was longer ago than you might think. I was in my twenties and living in Capernaum with my wife and her aging mother. We had moved there from Bethsaida where my family had lived for several generations. Andrew and I inherited the fishing boat from our father when he died. We were young, but we were strong and the lake provided us with a steady income.

Jesus and his mother and brothers and sisters moved to town one day and found a place to live not far from our house. They were a quiet family and very pleasant to be around. Jesus was a builder and carpenter, and soon began picking up small jobs helping neighbors with repairs to their doors and boats and carts and such. Apparently he had learned the skills of a carpenter from his father who, it seems, had died in a construction accident. It didn't take long for Jesus to get a reputation as a skilled and fair carpenter. He was always pleasant and really took a liking to the children wherever he went. He always had a little something he made or a pocket full of nuts to give to them before he finished a job. The kids really responded to him.

Jesus and I became friends and my wife and mother-in-law really enjoyed the company of his mother, Mary. Our families would often get together for the holidays. The women went to the well together almost daily to fill the cisterns. That chore required at least two trips back and forth to the well carrying those heavy jugs of water. My wife told me that one day Mary showed up pulling a small cart behind her that Jesus had made. The little cart just fit the water jar and made the task of collecting water so much easier for Mary. Several neighbors asked questions about the cart and a few put in orders for Jesus to make them one. But, and this may sound crazy, most folks turned their noses up at the idea saying that it was too new a concept and the old way had sufficed since the days of Abraham and was still good enough for today. But Jesus always had a mind for the future and how things could be made better for everyone, while most everyone seemed to think nothing could improve on the way things had always been done.

Since Jesus had grown up in the hills of central Galilee,

he had not spent much time around the water. He used to come down to the shoreline and sit and watch us clean the fish and repair the nets. We became friends during those afternoon conversations. Once or twice he even got in the boat and spent the evening out on the lake with us. As it would get dark, he would find a place in the bow to lie back and gaze up at the heavens. I never remember seeing him more peaceful than in those moments. Jesus and I were just about the same age, so we found a lot to talk about.

Interviewer: How did you happen to become one of his disciples?

Peter: One day, Jesus told us he was going to take his mother to visit her relative Elizabeth and his cousin John. They were gone for a couple of weeks. When they returned there was something different about him. That peacefulness I had seen come over him those nights when he would stretch out in the bow of the boat now seemed to be with him always. And yet, there was a new determination that replaced the laid-back attitude he had always had toward life.

It wasn't long after he came back that he came down to the shore one day while we were scraping barnacles off the boat. We had been fishing most of the night and had caught nothing. There was a small group of fishermen around. Jesus got into my boat and spoke to the folks for a few minutes; then he told me to row out a little way from the shore. I told him the fish weren't around at that time of the day, but I could tell he really wanted me to take the boat out.

We put out the nets and didn't have to wait long before they began to fill up. There were so many fish in the nets that our boat began to sink! I knew immediately that something unnatural had happened. I dropped to my knees and said, "Lord, I am just a sinner, why should you do this for me?" Jesus pulled me to my feet and said to Andrew and me, "Come on, come with me." "Where are you going?" I asked. "I'm going to teach you how to fish for people," he said with a sense of urgency and excitement in his voice.

"Leave the boat with your crew," he said, "You have trained them well. They can take care of the business while we are gone." "But what about your work and your mother?" I asked. Jesus replied, "I have left James in charge. He knows better than I do how to build things and he's got our younger brothers to help him. Are you with me?" Andrew and I looked at each other and nodded. Andrew said, "I'm ready for a change. How about you, brother?" As soon as we brought the boat ashore, we gave instructions to the first-mate. We had grown to trust Jesus and knew following him would be a safe thing to do.

The boat next to ours belonged to a man named Zebedee. His two boys, James and John heard what Jesus was saying and seemed interested. Jesus called out to them and said, "Come on men, I can use you, too." We didn't even take time to go home to pack a few necessities and say good-bye to the women – the crew members said they would do that for us. We went with Jesus to the synagogue where he prayed. After he prayed, we set out.

We stopped at a number of small villages along the way, and in each one, Jesus would go to the synagogue or place of prayer and engage the local villagers in conversations that always got around to him teaching from one of the prophets. I remember he always called the folks in those towns "neighbors" – no matter how far we were away from Capernaum. I had always thought neighbors were those who lived near us. But to Jesus, everyone was a neighbor. Many times there would be someone who was sick or disabled in some way. Jesus would go to that person, talk with them, pray with them, touch them and somehow, heal them. I didn't know how he did it, but I saw it with my own eyes!

At times, along the way, Jesus would invite others to join our group. Many declined for one reason or another, but some did join us and we all became enthusiastic followers of the teacher. Jesus became our rabbi and our friend and we became his disciples.

Interviewer: Can you tell us what it was like travelling with Jesus?

Peter: At first it was easy. He was so warm and genuine and really cared about all the people we were meeting. It wasn't long before they would invite us into their homes where they fed us and gave us a place to rest. There were a few nights when we laid down under the stars – but not many!

It seemed there was always someone who was sick or

in some other distress. Jesus would interrupt whatever his
plans were to spend time with them and remove whatever
demons were troubling them. Often they would bring the
sick to him on the Sabbath in the synagogue where they
knew he would be. There would always be great rejoicing
and singing when the families and the congregations
realized that their son or daughter was no longer sick.

Later, in our time together, as his reputation as a
healer spread, some of the more powerful rabbis began
to question his motives. According to them, healing on
the Sabbath was a form of work and was forbidden. For
Jesus it was not work. It was a gift he was always willing
to give. I remember this one time when a man with a
terribly injured hand was in the crowd at the back of the
synagogue. There were also some legal experts there who
seemed intent on catching Jesus breaking the Sabbath law
so they could bring charges against him.

Jesus saw the man. He also saw the lawyers. I saw
them all and was praying that Jesus would just let this one
go so we could get on our way with no trouble. But Jesus
had a different idea. He called the man with the damaged
hand to join him at the front. Then Jesus looked straight
at those lawyers and asked, "Is it legal on the Sabbath to
do good or to do evil? Is it right to save life or to destroy
it?" The room fell silent. Everyone knew that it was never
legal to do evil and, especially on the Sabbath, doing good
was the expected thing. And the commandments told us
that killing or destroying a life is not legal unless in case
of war or self-defense.

When the lawyers gave no response, Jesus told the

man to stretch out his hand. He did, and with no further words spoken, the hand was healthy, whole. Since Jesus had done nothing to affect the healing, the lawyers were furious that they had been outwitted. They immediately left the room, but we knew they were not through with Jesus and would be back.

The day soon came when there were too many people coming to him for him to teach them inside the synagogues. So he began to gather them on the hillsides around the lake.

On one particularly nice day, he walked up a small hill on the north side of the lake and sat down. Soon the whole mountainside was full of people eager to hear him teach. And brother, could he teach! He was always positive when he talked. He began that day by saying how the hopeless and the grieving and the humble, and the poor ought to be happy because God is looking after them and will comfort them. He encouraged all of us by saying that we are "the salt of the earth," and that we can change the world just like salt changes the meat. He said we can be lights to the world if we won't hide our joy and happiness. He told us so much more that day that it would take me a long time to repeat it all.

But what I really want to tell you is what happened after he finished preaching that day. It was getting late and the people were hungry. No one had brought anything much to eat, not thinking that they would be there that long. Jesus turned to the twelve of us and said simply, "Give them something to eat." We looked at each other realizing that we had not brought food for thousands of people. We started counting the little bit of coin we had and had to tell him that we didn't have enough to buy food for all of them. "No," he said, "I mean for you to feed them."

While we were scratching our heads trying to come up with a plan, but having no luck, a young boy tugged at my robe and said, "Mister, you can have the food my mother packed for me." I thanked the boy and I looked at what he was offering. I chuckled when I saw only five small loaves of bread and two fish. I thanked the boy again and turned to show Jesus what he had given. Jesus smiled and put his arm around the boy's shoulder. He took the food and offered a prayer of thanks to God and asked for a blessing for the boy.

Jesus then broke the bread and fish into pieces and gave it to us to disperse among the crowd. As we did so, we fully expected it not to go very far. But the more we handed out, the more was in our hands. Soon we were giving out larger portions but it never ran out. In fact, when everyone had eaten, someone began passing around empty baskets to collect the leftovers. You may not believe this, but they filled twelve baskets! It was the most miraculous thing I had ever seen! And that wasn't the only time that happened.

I remember another time. Jesus had said he needed to go away to pray. He asked James and John and me to come with him. We spent a day climbing in the mountains until we got to the highest peak in the area. He told the three of us to sit down and rest and he walked off a short distance and fell down in a posture of prayer. As we watched, it seemed that something changed in him. His face began to radiate light and his clothes appeared to flash as white as lightning!

Then two men appeared standing over him. Somehow we knew it was Moses and Elijah. The three of them spent some time talking while we watched, speechless. When it looked like the two men were about to leave, I jumped up and yelled out to Jesus that we could build three shelters, or altars, to commemorate the moment. I didn't know what else to say.

But as I was speaking, the fog moved in and covered the top of the mountain. We could see nothing, but we heard a voice. A big, booming voice that clearly said, "This is my Son, my chosen one. Listen to him." When the fog lifted, Jesus was standing alone. On the way down the mountain, Jesus asked that we not tell anyone what we had seen. "They won't understand," he said. Oh, how we wanted to tell the others, but Jesus was right, they wouldn't understand. They likely wouldn't really believe it anyway. But it happened and it convinced me beyond any doubt that Jesus was the Messiah the world had been looking for.

Interviewer: We would really like for you to tell us about the things Jesus taught. What do you remember about his message?

Peter: He was very clear in his teaching. His message was really very simple. You never had to scratch your head and wonder what he was getting at. He was mostly very positive and hopeful in the things he said. He talked a lot about getting along with other people – things like loving enemies, welcoming strangers, forgiving those who hurt you – things like that. Often he spoke in little stories, but they were always drawn from simple everyday things that even I could understand.

For example, he told a story about a man who was beat up and robbed while travelling from Jerusalem to Jericho. Now we all knew that for a Jew to travel alone was to invite trouble. Well, the robbers left the man on the road to die, which they thought would happen soon. A couple of really respectable Jewish leaders came to the place where the dying man lay, but because of previous appointments, they stepped over him and hurried away.

Then a Samaritan fellow came by. Now, no one who heard Jesus tell the story would have thought anything else but that the Samaritan would also pass the man on the road and do nothing, except maybe to spit on him or kick dirt into his wounds. But, as Jesus told the story, it was the Samaritan who stopped and knelt down and tried to bandage the man's wounds.

That small act of a Samaritan stopping to help a Jew would have been unreal enough for us to get the point that even a Samaritan could do something good. But Jesus went on and told how the Samaritan lifted the injured man onto his own animal and took him to the nearest place where he could be taken care of and rest. And then, Jesus added, that Samaritan paid the bill for the care offered and promised to come by in a day or two to check on the patient and pay whatever further costs may be incurred!

When he finished, he asked us, "Now, who was the neighbor to the wounded man?" The point, you see, was not that even a Samaritan can do something good now and then. The point was that being a neighbor involved going out of your way to help even someone no one would expect you to help. From that day on, whenever we heard Jesus talk about loving our neighbors, and we heard that a lot from him, I knew that he was including even Samaritans in that instruction.

He told another story that I always thought he was telling just for me. He talked about how a fishing net cast into the sea will gather up all manner of fish and how the Kingdom of Heaven is like that net. That there will be all kinds of people in the Kingdom of Heaven. At a later time, when we were trying to get the church going, I had that same message given to me again.

I had been invited to the home of a Roman Soldier to teach him about the message of Jesus. I knew the man was a Gentile and that, as a Jew, I was forbidden to go into his home and associate with him. While I was debating what to do, I received a vision of a large sheet coming down from heaven, and in that sheet were all the animals that Jews are forbidden to eat. In that moment, I heard the same booming voice that I had heard on the mountain top with Jesus. This time, the voice said, "Take something from the sheet and eat it!" At first I refused, but then the voice of God told me, "Peter, never consider unclean what God has made pure." After this happened three times, I finally got the message.

You see, it didn't matter at all to Jesus who you were, where you were from, how you spoke, who you loved – you were a brother or sister to him. He cared about you. He would help you however you needed help. He truly loved everyone and you could see it in the way he treated them.

I once asked Jesus about how to treat someone who was irritating me. I told him I had forgiven this person, but it didn't stop them from attacking me. He told me to forgive him again. So I asked him, "How many times must I forgive him? Seven times?" Jesus said, "No, Peter, not seven times but seventy times seven!" It took me a second to do the math, but eventually I realized what he meant was to stop counting and keep forgiving. That's the way he was. He held nothing against anyone. He just loved everyone.

Jesus taught us so much, but one of the last things he said to me I believe summed up all that he wanted us to know. This happened after he rose out of the grave. We were walking along the shoreline of the lake in Galilee when he asked me if I loved him. I was stunned because I thought surely he knew that we all loved him. That's why we had stayed with him. I said, "Yes, Lord, I love you." He responded by saying, "Then feed my lambs." As we walked along, I thought about what that might mean. Then he asked me the same question again, "Do you love me?" "Yes, Lord, I love you," I said. "Then take care of my sheep," was the reply that time. By the time he asked me a third time, "Do you love me?" and responded to my reply by saying, "Feed my sheep," I was beginning to get his point.

In that moment when he could have reminded me of anything he had ever taught us, he chose to tell me that what he wanted more than anything was for us to simply love people: to care for people, feed people, to look after the little ones and the weak ones. He knew there were things he had taught that confused us and that we argued about, but he wanted us to be absolutely clear that above anything else was that if we loved him, we should love the people he loved.

Interviewer: Thank you, Peter for sharing your memories of Jesus, and thank you for sharing those wonderful stories. Perhaps we could invite you back another day to tell us about that day when "he rose out of the grave" as you put it.

Peter: I would be most happy to do that.

Chapter 4

A Blind Man healed
Mark 8:22-26

ONE OF THE WAYS THE truth of God's love was revealed to the world was through the miracles of Jesus. In addition to miracles involving natural elements such as walking on water or turning water into wine, most of the miracles that are reported relate to the healing of individual persons such as casting out demons, restoring crippled limbs, restoring the ability to hear and see, curing sickness and even raising the dead.

The thing about those reports of persons receiving healing (and there are almost 50 of them in the gospels) is that in very few cases are we given any insight into who they were--not even their names. All of Christ's miracles provided dramatic and clear evidence that Jesus is the Son of God.

There are some dozen accounts in the gospels of Jesus healing blindness. None of those persons were named (except for Bartimaeus.) Their healings came in different ways. Blindness is a more physically dangerous handicap than deafness or the inability to speak or walk. The person who is blind is more dependent on the help of others to avoid danger, at least until they learn how to navigate for themselves. Even then, the blind person is vulnerable to the wicked intentions of those who would take advantage.

In this chapter, we will be introduced to one of those unnamed blind persons who encountered Jesus and explore what life might have been like before and after his healing.

Interviewer: Good morning sir. In Mark, chapter 8, the Bible gives us just a brief sketch of your encounter with Jesus, and we are hoping you could tell us more about yourself and about the day when Jesus restored your sight.

Blind man: Certainly. That was the most extraordinary day you can imagine!

I was born blind, though for the first years of my life, I didn't know what that meant. I knew that I lived with a woman and a man who, I learned from the words others used, were my mother and father. They loved me very much and tried to protect me from the dangers I couldn't see. I also knew there were people my same size who were called my brothers and sisters. One of the ways I began to learn about sight was when I would always bump into walls or into people, or I would stumble over tree roots or baskets, and people would say, "Look out! Can't you see that?" I wasn't sure what they meant, "can't you see", but I did notice that I seemed to be running into things a lot more than other people. I was sure that some of those times were the result of mean-spirited boys intentionally putting stones or other things in my path so they could laugh at me when I went tumbling down.

The way people talked about me made me realize that I was different. But I couldn't tell how it was that I was different. The way they laughed at me made me not like however it was that I was different. As I grew older I began to study my body to figure out who I was. I studied my face by running my hands over it. When I did that, I learned that the two flaps of skin on the side of my head they called ears were for hearing. When I covered them with my hands, noises became harder to hear, and when I cupped my hands next to them I could hear better. I found my mouth and I knew what I could do with it. And when I closed my nose with my fingers, it was obvious what it was for. But when I touched my eyes and explored them, I couldn't figure out what their use was. When I asked mother, she would just say, "They are for seeing." I didn't know what she was talking about.

Over time, I learned how to move around the house without knocking things over so much. I even learned how to get to the well and draw water and feed the animals in the yard. The more I spent time outside, the more the sand of the road would blow into my eyes and they would become infected and painful. And on very bright days when I could feel the heat of the sun strongly, my eyes would hurt. I still couldn't figure out what those eyes were for, but I learned to tie a cloth around my head to protect them. But that just made people notice me and gave people another thing to mock me about, so I learned to avoid people outside my family. I just kept to myself and was very lonely. I learned about things by holding them or smelling them or listening to them.

Because people always said that I looked different, I wanted to know what other people looked like. Did they also have ears and noses? When I asked my brothers what they looked like, they just laughed and said, "Why can't you see?" There was that word again. One day while we were playing, I caught my smaller sister and sat on her while I touched her face to figure out if she was the same as me. I ran my hands over her ears, her nose, her mouth (she bit me!) and her eyes. When I touched her eyes, she screamed as though I had hurt her. I hadn't meant to. My eyes didn't hurt when I touched them. I never could tell what other people looked like because no one outside my family would let me touch them.

Interviewer: Were there any positive things you remember about growing up?

Blind man: I always liked it when my father would take me with him to the synagogue for prayers. There would always be someone to tell us stories from the old days. I asked my father how he knew all those stories. Father said he was a rabbi and he was reading them from an old book. I didn't understand that either.

I especially liked the stories the rabbi told that were from the writings of a man named Isaiah. According to Isaiah, a day would come when "The people who walked in darkness would see a great light." – That's me I thought! He said, "A child called 'Wonderful Counselor and Mighty God' would lead them." He said there would come a day when, "the deaf will hear the words of a scroll and the eyes of the blind will see." He also said, "The glory of the Lord will appear and all people will see it together." I always got excited when I heard those stories and hoped I would know when that day came – and it did come!

Interviewer: What can you tell us about that day?

Blind man: For weeks, people on the street had been talking about a new teacher and healer who was going from town to town with a message of God's love for everyone. Some even speculated that he might be the one Isaiah had talked about coming from God. Then the word spread that he was coming to Bethsaida where I lived.

I made sure to sit out by the road in front of our house for the next several days so I didn't miss the chance to hear the teacher. The day came when I could hear a large crowd coming down the road. I asked what was happening, and someone said that Jesus was coming! As I sat there with my eyes covered because of all the dust in the air from the shuffling feet passing by, I listened but could not make out any one distinct voice. Then, just when it seemed the whole procession was on the road right in front of me, they all stopped and it got quiet.

As I tried to figure out what was happening, I could hear voices saying things like, "Rabbi, who sinned so that that man was born blind? Was it his parents' sin that caused this?" I knew they were talking about me and saying bad things about my parents. I began to yell back at them.

Suddenly two strong hands took hold of my arms and helped me to my feet--not in a rough way, but gently. As that was happening, the man who was helping me to stand answered them, "Neither this man nor his parents caused his blindness. This happened so that God's mighty works might be displayed in him."

I didn't say anything – I didn't know what to say. I didn't know what he meant by that, but I knew my parents were good people! But the man with the two strong arms said softly to me, "My name is Jesus and I would like to help you if would you would allow it." Not knowing what help he was offering, I just nodded my head in agreement to his offer and put out my hand to receive whatever coins he might put in it. He put his strong hand in my hand and led me away from the crowd to a quiet, shady place.

I may not have mentioned this before, but a person who is born without sight doesn't understand the importance of eye-to-eye contact when speaking with another person. We tend to move our head from side to side in a way that seems to the other person that we are not paying attention or not understanding. Actually, we are trying to find the best position to hear their voice clearly. The movement of our head is a way to pay close attention to their words.

When we stopped, Jesus stepped in front of me and stood facing me. He took my hands and moved them over his face so I could know what he looked like. His face was relaxed and felt kind. I nodded in appreciation. Then I could feel both his hands on my shoulders, slowly and gently moving up to my face. With his hands on my cheeks, he steadied my head. Then his hands moved up to cover my useless eyes. He held them there for a moment while he uttered a quick prayer.

Slowly he lifted his hands from my eyes and just stood there. After a moment, I blinked my eyelids and was startled by what happened. There was brightness and shapes! Some were moving, others were still. Then Jesus said, "Friend, do you see anything?" I said, "Yes. I see light and I see people." "What do the people look like?" he asked. "They just look like trees walking around," I answered. I thought that was what "seeing" was all about. I thought I was healed. I was so excited. I gave him a hug and thanked him and I started to dance around!

But then Jesus said, "Not so fast, my friend." And once again he raised his hands and covered my eyes with a firm but gentle pressure. When he lowered his hands and I blinked a couple times, things came into focus. I could see! Really see! The first thing I saw was the face of Jesus and it was beautiful. I looked all around and tried to take it all in. I could see the different shapes of the trees and the flowers on the short bushes. I could see that people weren't all the same. They were different sizes and colors, and had different faces.

As I stood there trying to comprehend all that I was seeing and all that had happened, I must have looked frightened because Jesus told me to go straight home and not try to go into the village.

That turned out to be crucial advice. For, you see, when a person who has never had sight suddenly sees, his mind is not prepared to comprehend all the new information that is sent to it. Things like depth perception, color variation, facial expressions--all can be disorienting to the newly sighted. The brightness of the afternoon sun was painful at first. It was best that I walked the familiar pathway to the house, and in the security of my own home learn how to handle my new-found ability to see.

Before I left, I asked Jesus why he stopped all those people just to help me. "I'm nobody," I said, "people have always told me that I am not worth anything. They say that it would be better for my parents if I had never been born. Some say that the devil must be in me and that I am evil. You must have more important things to do than pay attention to me."

In his gentle voice, Jesus said, "The people who have said those things to you are wrong. Your Father in heaven thinks you <u>are</u> someone of great worth and importance, and I have nothing more important to do than to help you. Go now and tell others what the Lord has done for you and praise the God of heaven for your sight. Go, rest, and I will check on you when I pass this way again." I went home and for the first time, I saw the beautiful faces of my loving mother and father.

Interviewer: Can you tell us what your life was like after that day?

Blind man: Well, at first it was very confusing. I was seeing things that I had only recognized by touch up to that point. Sometimes I had to close my eyes in order to recognize a vessel or tool that I was only familiar with by touch. And colors were amazing. I had heard people talk about colors, but I had no real understanding of what they were. I had decided that red was my favorite color. But when I could actually see the colors, red was not at all what I had thought it might be. I much prefer green.

Eventually, I started venturing out farther and farther. Most of the time I made my little sister go with me. The people of Bethsaida who had always known me as "the blind kid" avoided me for the most part, or thought I was trying to trick them into thinking that I could see. But there were those, a few, who trusted me and became my friends.

Interviewer: What was the most startling thing you learned?

Blind man: I learned that not everyone was blind! I never knew that. I also learned that there were people who couldn't hear or speak. When I was younger, I just thought that everyone was like me–living in darkness. When I got older I came to believe that I was the only one who could not see. Then I met another boy who was blind, and I came to realize that there are many who live in darkness. I wanted to help them regain sight or hearing or speech, whatever it was that was limiting their lives. I even tried touching that little boy's eyes, but he still couldn't see.

I asked and asked until I found out where Jesus was, and with my younger sister helping me, we found our way to him. I was able to get close to him not knowing if he would remember me. But he did. He was excited to see me. He called my name and grabbed me into a wonderful hug. He asked me how I was doing and then said, "I can see by the fact that you have come all this way that you must be doing well." I said yes and then told him of my concern about the other people I had met who were also limited in what they could do as I once was. I pleaded with Jesus to come back to Bethsaida and heal them.

He looked at me with tears in his eyes and said, "I heal people every day, wherever I go. But there are so many of them and I have a message to give to all people that is more important than just healing their bodies. I came to tell people that God loves them—all of them. I came to tell people that the happiness and peace they are hoping for in this world will be found not in armies or in riches or in fame, or even in healed bodies, but in loving God and each other and doing good to those who need it most."

I told him that once I had tried to heal a blind child in town, but when I touched him he still couldn't see. "How can I help him if I can't heal him?" I asked. Jesus said, "But you did help him. When you touched him, you helped him more than you know. You showed him that you could see him. That he is not invisible. You showed him that you know what he is experiencing. And because you thought he might be healed, you gave him hope that one day he might be healed. But most importantly, you let him know that he has a friend who cares about him."

Jesus told me that the gift I have to give is even better than the ability to heal. It is the gift of showing people that they are loved. That God loves them. That I love them. He told me to go back home and be a good friend to that boy. To make sure he feels love, and let others see you being a friend to one they so easily overlooked and judged.

I asked Jesus if I couldn't just stay with him. He said, "No, there is someone at home who needs your love and friendship. Now go. Go in peace and in love, and the God of peace and God's eternal love will go with you."

I did return home, and over the next months, I began to realize that the greatest gift I had received was not the ability to see, but the ability to serve. People began bringing their sons and daughters to me just to show them that a boy who was once blind now could see. Just by my talking to them and telling them about Jesus, who doesn't condemn them but who loves them, those kids seemed to gain hope.

There were so many who came to me to talk about the things that scared them or were preventing them from moving forward. Not just the blind, but the crippled and the deaf as well. Some had no outward signs of any problems but they would open their hearts and tell me about the things that were tearing them down from the inside. As they talked, I listened. I mostly listened, wondering if I would have any helpful words for them. But most often, when they finished, before I could say anything, they thanked me for listening and said that was the first time anyone cared enough to just listen to their story.

Interviewer: We thank you for your time today and for telling us your story.

Blind man: Before we go, I would like to share some very precious words from the prophet Isaiah that have long been an inspiration to me. Where Isaiah is describing the Messiah that God promised to send to us, he said:

> "Here is my servant, the one I uphold. [He] will grasp your hand and guard you, [He will be] a covenant to the people and a light to the nations, to open blind eyes, to lead the prisoners from prison, and those who sit in darkness from the dungeon.
>
> I am the Lord; that is my name. I will make the blind walk a road they don't know, and I will guide them in paths they don't know. And I will turn darkness before them into light and rough places into level ground. These things I will do; I won't abandon them. (Isaiah 42:1, 6-8, 16)

I never was able to help anyone who was blind to see, but I have seen the miracle of hope bringing light into the lives of many when they first heard that God loves them and doesn't condemn them. I have witnessed lives changed not because bodies were healed, but because hearts were comforted by a simple word of acknowledgment and friendship.

Interviewer: Thank you.

Chapter 5

A Samaritan Woman
at the well
John 4:1-42

THIS INTERVIEW IS WITH ONE about whom we know more personal information than most anyone else in the New Testament. We don't know her name, but from the information we have, we can piece together a fairly detailed sketch of her life. Listen as she tells the story of her encounter with Jesus.

Interviewer: Good morning Ma'am. We appreciate your time and are excited to hear your memories of the day you met Jesus. Can you begin by telling us a little about yourself and that amazing moment when you encountered the Lord?

Samaritan woman: Sure. To begin, the thing that makes this story so amazing is that I am a Samaritan woman and Jesus was a Jewish man. Do you know why that is so amazing?

Interviewer: About all we know is that there was some sort of conflict between Jews and Samaritans. Perhaps you could explain what that was all about and how it all got started?

Samaritan woman: Let me tell you the story the way I learned it. It all started 1,000 years ago with King Solomon. Solomon's father, the great King David, built the kingdom of Israel by defeating the Philistines. Solomon expanded the kingdom until it reached from Egypt to the Euphrates River. Solomon built the Temple, the palace, the hall of justice, and the wall around Jerusalem. It took 20 years to build all that plus the cities for storing grain and the cities used for storing the chariots and cavalry.

The problem was that Solomon built all that he built on the backs of the forced labor of our own people. All the men were divided up into labor gangs.

Then Solomon died and his son Rehoboam was crowned king in Jerusalem. But since ten of the ancient tribes lived up north, Rehoboam and his men traveled up north so the northerners could meet him and have a coronation ceremony for him there as well. However, before that could all be arranged, a delegation of the elders from the northern tribes met with the new king and said, "Look, your father made our workload very hard for us. If you will just lessen the demands your father placed on us and lighten the heavy workload he demanded from us, then we will serve you."

Rehoboam answered them, "Come back in three days and I will give you my answer." When Rehoboam consulted with the senior advisors who had advised his father, they said, "If you will be a servant to this people by answering them and speaking good words today, then they will be your servants forever."

But Rehoboam ignored the advice the elders gave him and instead sought the counsel of his young friends who had grown up with him. "What do you advise," he asked them, "should I cut them a break?" The young advisors said to him, "These people said to you, 'Your father made our workload heavy; lighten it for us.' But here's what you <u>should</u> say to them, 'My baby finger is thicker than my father's entire waist! So if my father made your workload heavy, I'll make it even heavier! If my father disciplined you with whips, I'll do it with scorpions!'" And that is what Rehoboam told the northern tribes.

When the northern elders returned after three days for Rehoboam's answer, they were incensed and told Rehoboam to "go back to his own home in the south – but he better keep looking over his shoulder because they were now his enemies. King Rehoboam quickly got into his chariot and fled to Jerusalem. Israel has been in rebellion against the house of David to this day. The kingdom in the south came to be known as Judah.

Interviewer: But that was so long ago! Why hasn't that rift been healed?

Samaritan woman: That's a fair question. About 300 years after those events, the kingdom of Assyria overran our little kingdom of Israel, also known as Samaria, since that was our capitol city. They removed large segments of the population and replaced them with captives from other nations.

Naturally, over time, the Jews remaining in Samaria intermarried with their foreign neighbors and had children that were of mixed blood. Later, when the kingdom of Babylon captured the area of Judah to the south, they sent practically all of that population into exile in Babylon. When the Persians conquered the Babylonians, they allowed the captive Jewish population to return to the lands around Jerusalem.

When those returned Jews began to rebuild the city and the temple, people from the north offered to help since that had been our temple at one time as well. But those offers to help were rejected because, as we were told, we had "polluted the blood of Abraham with our marriages to non-Jewish people." And since God had called the Jews his "Chosen People," the southerners believed mixed-race people were not good enough to be God's "holy nation." So our ancestors chose Mt. Gerizim as the place for our altar. We have been worshipping there ever since.

Of course, many of us Samaritans find it funny that Samaria lies right between Galilee in the north and Judea in the south. Galilean Jews traveling to Jerusalem three times a year for their festivals have to walk right through our territory, or take a much longer route across the river. Samaritan young people get a kick out of harassing the Jewish travelers.

But let me get back to that day at the well.

Interviewer: Yes, please.

Samaritan woman: I noticed a man sitting alone on the bench near the well. But I looked away and went about my chore of drawing water. It was the middle of the day and the sun was extremely hot. I sensed that the man was looking at me, so I turned and said, rather abruptly, "What do you want?" The man said, "Sister, I have come a long way and I am very thirsty. Could you please give me a drink of water?" He said, "My friends have gone into town to buy some food, but I chose to rest here a while and I am truly thirsty."

I looked at him long enough to figure out that he was not a Samaritan, but Jewish. So I said, "How dare you, a Jewish man, ask for something to drink from me, a Samaritan woman!"

When he responded, his voice was soft and calm, and not in the least threatening. I wasn't sure what he meant when he said, "If you recognized God's gift and who is saying to you, 'Give me some water to drink,' you would be asking him and he would give you living water."

Half confused and half irritated, I pointed out the obvious to him, "Sir, you don't even have a bucket and this well is deep. Where are you going to get that living water or water of any kind? You don't think that you are greater than our father Jacob, do you? Jacob gave this well to us, and he drank from it himself, as did his sons and his livestock."

Jesus answered, "Everyone who drinks this water will be thirsty again." "You've got that right!" I said. "But whoever drinks from the water that I will give will never be thirsty again, he said. "The water that I give will become a spring of water that bubbles up into eternal life in those who drink it."

I wasn't exactly sure what he was talking about, but it sounded like I wouldn't have to trudge back and forth to this well twice a day if I had that water. So I said, "Sir, give me this water so that I will never be thirsty and will never need to come here to draw water!" I don't know what I was expecting to happen next, but I was not prepared for what he said.

Jesus said, "Woman, go and get your husband and bring him back here."

Since I was living with a man at the time but was not officially married, I said, "I don't have a husband." Just about the time when I had decided that Jesus didn't really know what he was talking about, he said, "You are right in saying that you don't have a husband right now. You've had five husbands and the man you are living with now isn't your husband. You have spoken truthfully."

"What are you, some kind of prophet," I asked? "How could you know all that about me?" Then I said, "If you are such a prophet, tell me who is right – our people who worship here on Mt. Gerizim or your people who worship in Jerusalem?"

Again, his answer was strange. He said, "The time is coming when you and your people will not worship on this mountain or in Jerusalem." He said, "The time is coming when true worshippers will worship in spirit and in truth. This is the way the Father wants you to worship him – in spirit, not in rule and law. God is spirit, and it is necessary to worship God in spirit and in truth."

I didn't know what to say to that, so I said, "Well, I know the Messiah is coming. When he comes, he will teach everything to us."

Then Jesus said, "Woman, I am the Messiah."

"That's a mighty big claim to make," I said.

Just then, his friends returned with the food they had purchased. When they saw him talking to me, they were obviously unsettled. I didn't stay around to hear what they would say. I set down my water jar and ran back into town and called for people to come out and see this man who had told me everything I had ever done. "He is claiming to be the Messiah," I said, "Could it really be?" It didn't take much for a crowd to gather and start heading toward the well.

After listening to Jesus for a while you could feel people responding to what he taught. Before sundown, the leaders of the Samaritans invited Jesus to come and stay with them. And he did! He stayed for two whole days! Eventually some of the villagers told me that they had only gone out to see Jesus because of the wild story I had told them. But they said that after listening to him, they had come to believe for themselves that Jesus must surely be the savior the world needed!

While he was with us, he told us again and again that the God of our ancestors is the God of the whole world and of everyone in it. He said that God doesn't favor anyone because of their nation or their way of worship or their place of worship. He said that in God's eyes, there are no worthy or unworthy ones; no shackled slaves or privileged rich ones. He said that women were just as important and valuable to God as were men. He said we should love everyone as much as we love ourselves.

When someone said, "But sir, the Jews are our enemies. You can't expect us to love them after how they have treated us these many years."

Jesus responded by reminding us that the Jews were our brothers and sisters, and that loving them could be the way out of this hostility. He told a story about a Jewish man who was robbed on the road to Jerusalem. In his story, two or three Jewish priests and lawyers came to the place where the dying man was lying on the road. They all passed by him because they were too busy to stop or they didn't want to dirty themselves by assisting the man. But then he said that a Samaritan man came by and stopped to give aid. He said that Samaritan lifted the Jewish man onto his own donkey and took him to the nearest inn where he could be nursed to health. He paid the innkeeper for the room and before he left, he promised that he would return to pay whatever additional expenses there might be.

When he finished the story, he told us not to waste time figuring out who are our neighbors and who our enemies are, but, "To spend our time being a neighbor to everyone and then you can count them as your friends."

Later, as I thought back to my encounter with Jesus at the well, I realized what it was that had drawn me to him. When he was talking about all the failed relationships in my life and what a mess I had made of things, he was not judging me. He never condemned me for my mistakes. And, when I realized that he knew all that stuff about me when he first asked me for a drink of water, I knew that it didn't make any difference to him who I was or what I had done. He was willing to talk with me and to drink from my ladle.

Interviewer: Did you ever learn what happened to Jesus after that day?

Samaritan woman: In the months that followed, we heard of the many fantastic things Jesus was doing. We heard not only of the many healings he did, but of the times when he stood up to the Temple officials because of how they were perverting the faith with their rules. Then we began to hear rumors that Jesus had been crucified, but that he came out of his grave - still alive!

Not long after that, we began to see a lot of people coming into Samaria from Jerusalem. Remembering what Jesus had said about the Samaritan man who cared for the Jewish man and how it was more important to be a neighbor than to turn people away, we tried to help those "neighbors" find places to stay and ways to get settled. As we got to know them, we discovered that they were followers of Jesus, just as we were.

Our new friends told us about what was happening to the believers in Jerusalem. They said people were turning against them. That there was a man named Saul going around arresting and jailing the followers of Jesus. They had killed some leaders of the church and were trying to shut the whole thing down!

One day, one of the men who had been with Jesus when he stayed in our village came back to check on our fellowship and to tell us more of the good news that Jesus had been spreading. This man, Philip, I think was his name, not only was a great preacher, but he had the power to heal many of our sick. People who had unclean spirits would shriek as those spirits came out of them. Some who had been paralyzed or crippled were healed. Those were great days!

When word reached the other friends of Jesus in Jerusalem that people in Samaria were coming to believe in Jesus, two more of the leaders came to help out. Their names were Peter and John. We had been told by Philip that if we were really wanting to turn away from our sinful ways, we should pour water over our heads as a symbol of the washing away of evil desires and practices. Philip called that "baptism." Peter and John said there was another, even more important "baptism" that we should receive. They said it was for us to let the power of God's own spirit wash over us.

When they laid their hands on me, something happened! I felt something. I felt joy. I felt loved. I felt strong. I felt so many things I can't list them all. But from that moment, I knew that God had not only touched me, but that God had something for me to do.

The fellowship of those of us who followed the way Jesus taught kept growing as more and more people began to listen to the teaching of the power of love to turn enemies into friends, and the joy we each received when we were helping someone with a problem they had. Some of our group wanted to leave the village and go to tell Samaritans in other towns about Jesus. And some did. But from the moment when I received the power of God's spirit, I never wanted to leave my town and family. I was able to find plenty to do to teach the children and help the women.

Many years later, when I was an old woman, I was drawing water from that same well when a group of Jewish men came by. I quickly offered them water from my ladle and invited them to come into town and get some food. One of the men who seemed to be a leader stepped forward and introduced himself to me.

"My name is Paul," he said, "you may have heard of me. I used to go by the name of Saul." I gasped when I heard that! He went on to say that once he tried to silence the church of Jesus, but for many years now, after meeting Jesus, he had been travelling far to spread the good news of God's love and of the forgiving love of Christ Jesus. He said that meeting Jesus had changed his life, and he believed that spreading the name of Jesus across the nations could change the world. He asked me if I had ever met Jesus.

"Yes," I said, "I met him right here at this well when he asked me for a drink of water, and he changed my life as well." Paul thanked me for my hospitality and prayed for our people before the group moved on toward Jerusalem.

As I watched them walk away, I remembered what

Jesus had once told me: that he could give me water from a never-ending stream; and I knew that I had been drinking from that living spring ever since I came to know Jesus.

Interviewer: Wow! What a fantastic story you have told us, and how thankful we are to have been able to hear you tell it. Thank you so very much.

Chapter 6

Philip, the Evangelist
John 14:8-11

IN THIS CHAPTER, WE WILL be interviewing one of the twelve disciples of Jesus. Nothing at all is said about Philip in the gospels of Matthew, Mark or Luke except that his name is included in the lists of the 12. In the gospel of John, there are two stories where Philip is featured, albeit briefly. A man named Philip is also mentioned in the Book of Acts, and some have identified that man as possibly being the disciple, Philip. There is also a man named Philip in the list of the seven deacons. Though there is no evidence that the deacon Philip was the same as the disciple Philip, neither is there any reason not to suppose that he could have been. Because the seven deacons were chosen to deal with controversies that included some Greek believers, and Philip the disciple was likely Greek, I am going to base part of this interview on that supposition.

Interviewer: Philip, you are the only one of the twelve disciples with a Greek name. Can you tell us why your parents chose your name? Is there any significance behind it?

Philip: In my time there was always a meaning to a name. Yes, Philip is a strong Greek name, going back to the father of Alexander the Great – Philip of Macedon. But more recently, Philip, son of the great and cruel Herod, was the governor of our region of Galilee, and had been for some time when I was born. He had proved himself not to be anything like his father. He was fair and honest in his dealings with his subjects, and compassionate, as much as a king might have been. He had also invested a great deal in rebuilding Bethsaida, my hometown. Eventually, Bethsaida became the capital of the province and something of a center of trade. My parents, as with many others, wishing to honor the governor and perhaps gain his favor in their businesses, named me Philip after our town's benefactor. Consequently, there were many boys my age named Philip in my school. By the way, "Philip" means "lover of horses."

Interviewer: Did you own horses?

Philip: No, no! Only Romans could own or ride horses. They are beautiful animals, though.

Interviewer: Indeed. Well, can you tell us how you came to know Jesus?

Philip: I had been a follower of the John who called people to be baptized in the river. I was there the day

Jesus came to the river and presented himself to John for baptism. At the end of that day, a group of us who were disciples of John were sitting around the fire and listening to Jesus. He spoke with such understanding and knowledge about the Heavenly Father. I was immediately drawn to him. During our conversation, he said he was preparing to go into the villages of Galilee to teach. John could tell from my expression that I wanted to go with Jesus, and he gave me permission to follow him. Before I could say anything to Jesus, Jesus came to me and said, "I need you to follow me, Philip."

I went and found my friend Nathanael and told him, "We have found the one Moses wrote about in the Law and the Prophets. His name is Jesus. He is the son of the carpenter Joseph, from Nazareth." Nathanael, who had never been the most positive personality, responded in a way that didn't really surprise me. What he said was what most people said, or at least thought about people from Nazareth. He said, "Can anything good come out of Nazareth?" What he was referring to was the general feeling that Nazareth was a town of mostly tradesmen and laborers, and was quite a rough place to be – especially after dark!

I said, "Nathanael, just come and see."

As we approached the place where Jesus was waiting, Jesus said, "Now here is a genuine Israelite who can never tell a falsehood." Nathanael was surprised and asked him, "How do you know me?" Jesus said, "Nathanael, even before Philip called you, I saw you sitting under that fig tree."

Nathanael was flabbergasted and said, "Rabbi, you are truly the Son of God and the king of Israel!"

Jesus chuckled and said, "Whoa, Nathanael! Do you believe just because I said I saw you under a tree? Wow, you are easily impressed. Just wait though and you will see much greater things than that. You are going to see heaven open and God's angels going up to heaven, and coming down to earth on the Son of Man." Those were mystical words that intrigued both Nathanael and me, so we fell in with the group around Jesus and off we went.

Interviewer: Can you tell us where you went?

Philip: One of the first places we stopped when we got to Galilee was the village of Cana. As we entered the village, it was obvious from all the excitement and decorations around the town that there was going to be a wedding. We met Jesus' mother who was there, and Jesus said we were all invited to the banquet. At one point during the feast, I noticed all the servants looking very distressed. There was a lot of whispering back and forth among them, and then to the bride's father. I could tell something was wrong.

Actually it was Jesus' mother who figured out what the problem was. It seems they had run out of wine! If that word got around, it would have been taken as a serious insult to the wedding guests. Jesus' mother leaned over to him and whispered something in his ear at which point he got up and left the table.

Nathanael and I watched as Jesus went over to the servants and instructed them to fill the six empty wine jars with water. Now these jars were the large amphorae from which the smaller table pitchers were filled. They each held about twenty or thirty gallons.

Then Jesus told the servants to present the six jars of water to the headwaiter, which they did. The headwaiter took a ladle and sampled the contents of each jar. He looked shocked and pleased from what we could tell. They served the new wine and the celebration continued well into the night. At some point in the night, I noticed the headwaiter approach the groom and say to him, "Sir, I've supervised many of these parties, but I've never seen anyone serve the inferior wine first and then bring out the superior vintages. Well played!" The groom looked perplexed, but I knew what had happened. Finally, close to dawn, we left the wedding party and with Mary, Jesus' mother, by his side, we all headed down to Capernaum where we stayed for several days.

I know that Jesus never said anything to anyone about what he had done by turning the water into wine at the wedding. But I knew and Nathanael knew. We saw the loving thing he had done for that couple to save them from a great embarrassment, and we knew that he didn't make a show of it so everyone would look at him. He wanted no credit. But those of us who witnessed the event were impressed, and we came to believe even more that Jesus had a special power from God.

I want to tell you about another time when a simple question Jesus asked me gave me a deeper insight into his way of thinking. We had just crossed the sea in Galilee after Jesus had healed many people. The people wouldn't let Jesus out of their sight. As we sailed, they ran around the shoreline and were there when we docked the boat. Jesus knew that by having the people sit on the hillside and standing with his back to the water the people would be able to hear him better.

We were all tired. After Jesus talked to the crowd for a long time, it was getting late in the afternoon. The people were tired and hungry. Jesus turned specifically to me and asked me, "Philip, where will we buy enough food to feed all these people?" I think he asked me that question to test me. He knew that I could be something of a literalist.

But I took his bait. Quickly, in my head, I calculated approximately what the cost would be, at current prices, to purchase that volume of food, and it was no small number. "Jesus," I said, "it will take more than six months wages to buy that quantity of food. And the logistical problems of getting it prepared and distributed will be impossible. It can't be done." Jesus smiled.

At just that time, Andrew showed up leading a young boy. The boy had offered Andrew his lunch which consisted of five loaves of barley bread and two small fish. When Andrew offered it to Jesus, I blurted out, "This is a joke! That's not nearly enough. That's not going to feed a crowd like this." Jesus gave me a stern look and said, "Philip, have the people sit down," and he offered a prayer of thanksgiving for the boy and for the gift he offered and asked God to bless that bread and those little fish until they were enough.

There were thousands on that hillside – maybe even 5,000! Jesus didn't hesitate. He broke the loaves and fish into pieces and handed some to each of us to distribute. It was such a small amount! I didn't know what to do, so I just held my hands out and let the people take however much they wanted. What happened next was unreal! As I went from person to person, they each took some food and each time they did there was more in my hands than before! When it became obvious that everyone would be fed, people began taking larger amounts. And they all saw what was happening – the food just kept expanding in my hands. The same was happening with the others as well!

When everyone had eaten their fill, Jesus told us to "gather up the leftover pieces so nothing would be wasted." We got baskets and started circulating among the crowd again. When we were done, each of our baskets were filled. It began to sink in to the minds of the people that they had just witnessed a most miraculous event, and they began to say, "This is truly the prophet that God has sent into the world!"

As their enthusiasm built and certain voices began calling for them to make Jesus into a king, Jesus realized that before things got out of hand it would be best for him to slip away. He left us there to deal with the crowd while he went off alone up in the mountains.

Jesus was always doing things like that – feeding hungry people, curing sick people, and standing up for the innocent. On those many occasions when some big shot from Jerusalem accused him of "working on the Sabbath," or of breaking some obscure old law that made no difference to anyone, or even of being possessed by the devil, Jesus never backed down. He always took the side of the needy. He always said that he was only doing what God wanted him to do and what God wanted us to do for each other.

Interviewer: Is there anything else you would like to add?

Philip: Yes, I'd like to tell you about a couple of things that happened the last time we went to Jerusalem, if I may.

Interviewer: Certainly. Please do.

Philip: The day we arrived in Jerusalem for the final time was a day of great commotion. In addition to the normal crowds of pilgrims who were arriving for the Passover, there was a crowd of several hundred that had attached themselves to Jesus. As we came down the hill from Bethany, they began to gather palm branches and wave them overhead shouting, "Here comes the king of the Jews!" I know that the Roman and Jewish observers were watching us, but thankfully the followers remained peaceful, so there was no cause for intervention.

At some point along the way, I was approached by some Greek fellows who were headed to the temple to worship. They must have been told my name and assumed I was Greek. They spoke to me in Greek which I barely understood. When I indicated that I didn't understand their language, they said, in very rough Aramaic, "Sir, we want to see Jesus and we have been told that you are close to him." I found Andrew and together we brought those men to Jesus. Jesus spoke to them and blessed them by putting his hand on their heads.

Then Jesus thanked me for bringing those strangers to meet him. I said it was nothing, no need for thanks to which Jesus replied, "Oh, but Philip, it was something! Many people are hungry for something to feed their souls and I have come to feed them. But how are they going to find me unless someone like you leads them to me?" As I thought about all the things the others in our group could do – teaching, preaching, healing -- I knew I could do none of those things well. In fact, I had always wondered why Jesus let me stay around. I never seemed to have much to contribute. But when he said that he needed people like me who could invite people to him. I knew that was easy for me to do.

Interviewer: Can you tell us about what happened the night you shared the Passover feast with Jesus?

Philip: After the supper, Jesus was saying some things that I didn't completely understand. He talked about going away to the Father's house and then returning for us, and that we would know the way. Thomas said, "Lord, we don't know where you are going, how can we know the way?"

What Jesus said next, I clearly remember. He said he was the way, the truth and the life. "No one comes to the Father except through me," he said. "If you have really known me, you will know the Father. From now on you know him and have seen him." That's when I had to interrupt him. We had long been hoping he would introduce us to the Father. All we really wanted was to see God so we could describe him when others asked us what he is like. So, I said, "Lord, show us the Father; that will be enough; that's all we ask."

Jesus said to me, "Don't you know me, Philip? Have I been with you all this time and you haven't figured it out yet? Whoever has seen me has seen the Father. Don't you believe that I am in the Father and the Father is in me? We are the same. The words that I have spoken – they are not my words but the Father's. The works that I do are the works the Father is doing through me. Believe me because of the works you have seen me do. I am going to the Father, so I need you to stay here to keep doing the works you have seen me do. If you will work in my name, you will do even greater things than you have seen me do."

"Lord," I replied, "What work can I do? I'm not a clear speaker; I'm not a healer; and I'm no scholar who can recite all the laws. What can I possibly do to help you?"

"You can keep inviting people to meet me," said Jesus, "just like you invited Nathanael, and now these Greek men."

"But what do I tell them, Lord?"

"Do you remember what I told those young men who wanted to know what they had to do to get into heaven when they claimed to be keeping all the laws?" Jesus asked.

"Yes," I said, "You told them to love God and to love everyone else."

"That's right," he said. "If you love me you will have kept all my commandments. And whoever loves me will be loved by the Father. We will come to that person and make our home with them."

"But, if you are going away, how will we know if we are doing the right things?" I said. Jesus said to all of us, "Don't worry, I will not leave you like orphans with no one to look after you. The Father is preparing to send another helper to be with you. In fact, the Father is going to come to you himself in Spirit and will stay with you. The Spirit of the Father will speak to you and remind you of all that I have taught you. Through his Spirit the Father will guide you and will counsel you in the right things to do and the right ways to go."

Before we left that upstairs room, Jesus said, "I don't want your hearts to be troubled and I don't want you to worry or be afraid. I want you to be at peace. I want you to have the strong peace of knowing that you are not alone and that there is nothing that can stand between you and the love of the Father who is in Heaven."

Things sort of went downhill after that, what with the arrest in the garden, the mock trial with bribed witnesses, the sentence of death and the suffering on the cross. It was all so unjust, so cruel. But through all those dark hours I couldn't stop hearing him say, "I will not leave you orphaned. I want you to be at peace." I remained distraught right up to the moment on the first day of the week when the women came rushing into the room telling us that he wasn't in the grave!

In that moment, we didn't really know what had happened, but I knew that we were not alone and the

Father would lead us out of those dark moments back into the light and the peace we had known when he was with us!

Interviewer: We know that you were part of the first organizing of the church. Could you share with us what it was like in the first months after Jesus rose and ascended into heaven? What part did you play in those first days of the Christian movement?

Philip: Those were truly exciting and challenging days. People kept coming to hear the good news that we had to share. Many stayed and joined the constantly growing fellowship of believers – and not just Jews. We were welcoming Greeks, Ethiopians, and Romans – people from all over! It got to the point when the details of feeding and caring for all those people were limiting the time the twelve of us had to teach.

One source of tension that arose was between the Greek-speaking believers and the Aramaic-speaking believers. The Greek speakers were complaining that their family members, specifically their widows, were not being treated fairly in the food distribution. It was clear something had to be done.

We had a meeting, and it was decided that we needed to appoint a committee to take charge of those matters. We decided to select seven men for the job, and because I spoke a little Greek, it was decided that I should be one of the seven. They thought that I could act as a liaison to the others. I also think it was because Jesus had chosen me to handle the food distribution on the hill that day, so they thought I had experience in food management. The others were Stephen, Prochorus, Nicanor, Timon, Parmenasm, and Nicolaus. Once we got to work, things began to run more smoothly.

I know you have heard the story of what happened to Stephen. He was a particularly gifted young man. God had gifted him with exceptional powers of preaching and healing. It didn't take long before some jealous members of the synagogue brought him up on some ridiculous charges like insulting Moses and God. They brought him before the Jerusalem Council of priests, and after Stephen gave a magnificent defense of his faith, they had him stoned to death. The way he spoke about God's faithfulness to his people from Abraham and Moses to David and Jesus was beautiful. With his dying breath, he echoed Jesus' last words by asking God to forgive even those who were killing him.

Following the death of Stephen, a Pharisee named Saul began to harass the church. That man was later chosen by God to lead the church into the greater world. But because of his activities at the first, the believers began to scatter. I went to Samaria and began to preach. There were many there who remembered when Jesus had stayed with them and many more came to believe in Jesus as the Christ. Even Peter and John had to come to Samaria to see the wonderful things that were happening there.

Not long after that, an angel from the Lord spoke to me and told me to take the road that leads from Jerusalem to Gaza through the desert. While on that lonely road, wondering what I was to do, a very fancy carriage passed me. From the colors and markings, I could assume it was from Africa somewhere. The Spirit of God spoke to me and told me to catch up with the carriage and speak to the man inside.

Turns out he was the official treasurer to the Queen of Ethiopia, and he was reading a copy of our scriptures that he had acquired while he was in Jerusalem. When I introduced myself, I realized that he was reading from the book of Isaiah. I asked him if he understood what it was that he was reading. He confessed that, without someone to guide him, he was having trouble understanding. He invited me to sit in his carriage with him and teach him, which I gladly did.

The eunuch asked me who Isaiah was talking about when he described the child who would bear all authority on his shoulders and who would have the Lord's spirit resting on him. Using those verses as a starting point, I told him the whole story about Jesus. When I got to the part about the resurrection from the dead, the Ethiopian said, "I want to be one of that man's followers. What do I have to do?"

There was a small spring in the desert there and I led the man into the water and poured water over his head invoking the name of the Father and the Son and the Holy Spirit. You should have seen the look of pure joy on that man's face as the water ran down over his entire body.

As that man travelled on to take the good news story of Jesus back to Africa, God redirected me northward toward Caesarea. In Caesarea, I continued to teach about Jesus and God's wondrous love to all people. We developed quite a fellowship of believers there over time.

I eventually settled down in Caesarea and started a family. My wife and I had four daughters who, as they grew, each became involved in the ministry of that church. Many years later when the girls were in their teens, I finally got the chance to meet the man who was responsible for the scattering of the church in the first place. When I first knew about him, he was called Saul. Now he was Paul and was the greatest evangelist the church had at that time. Paul stayed with my family for several days before going on to Jerusalem.

Accompanying Paul at that time was a young Greek doctor named Luke. He was a sensitive young man and was terribly interested in having me tell him the stories about Jesus since I had walked with him. He said he was working on putting together a book about Jesus' life and teachings and he wanted it to be "an orderly account." I told him all I could remember and then advised him to seek out Peter and John in Jerusalem for more details.

Well, that's probably enough for now. It has been a privilege talking to you.

Interviewer: Thank you so much, Philip, for sharing such personal and inspiring memories.

Chapter 7

John Mark, an eyewitness
Mark 14:51, Acts 12:25

IN THIS CHAPTER, OUR INTERVIEW will be with a young man named John Mark, most commonly known by just his second name, Mark. Mark was not one of the twelve disciples who spent months or years with Jesus. Yet Mark wrote the first of the biographies of Jesus that we call "Gospels." Who was he? Where did he get his information that was so accurate that more than 80% of his words were copied directly by Matthew and Luke? Since he is never mentioned in his own gospel account, how do we know anything about him – even his name? What part did he play in the early church? These and other questions we hope to answer as we interview John Mark.

Interviewer: John Mark, it is a pleasure to have you with us today.

Mark: Please just call me Mark.

Interviewer: Very well. Since you wrote the earliest of the four gospel accounts of Jesus' life that are preserved in the Bible of the Christian church, but there is no record of you having travelled with Jesus, we are interested in knowing if you ever met Jesus in person and how did you come by your information about his ministry?

Mark: Well, those are two very interesting questions. This may take a while. I hope you have time.

Interviewer: Please, take all the time you need.

Mark: Very well then. My father was a rather successful trader in commodities in his time - wines and spices and locally produced cloths. He travelled a lot, mostly up into and through Samaria and Galilee and, at times, into Syria. He would always come home with stories to tell of people he met and things he had seen. My mother, whose name was Mary, and I were always excited when he returned, and I could tell my mother was greatly relieved since travelling at that time, even with a retinue of servants with you, was a risky if not downright dangerous thing to do.

After one trip, father told us about a wonderful new teacher he had come across. He said he had followed a growing crowd of people along the edge of the great lake in Galilee. They were all following this one man who led them to sit on the side of a hill. Father said, "I was able to get close enough to hear what the teacher said that day and it was surprising, amazing, and comforting all at the same time." He said the man's name was Jesus.

"He spoke to the things that were hurting people," father said. Hunger, hatreds, fears, Romans. He said that there was hope coming for the grieving, the poor, the persecuted, for everyone. He said there was a new kingdom coming – a new kind of kingdom, the kingdom of God! He said the kingdom of God will be like a seed. It starts out as this tiny little speck of a seed, but once it is planted and starts growing, it grows into such a large tree that all the birds of the sky can find room to build their nests among its branches. He said the kingdom of God will be big enough to include Jews and Romans and Samaritans and Greeks and everyone else who obeys his commandments.

I asked what his commandments were. "Are they different from the commandments of Moses?" I asked. My father told me Jesus said that they were no different from Moses' commands, just stated in more positive words. He said that instead of listing all the things we are forbidden from doing, Jesus gave a list of the things God wants us to do – and it was a short list. Just two things. "Love the Lord God with all that you are and all that you have." That was the first thing on the list. The second thing is to "Love your neighbor, your enemy, and yourself."

Mother said, "That's all? Just love God and love people?" "That's all," dad said.

"I want to go hear him," I said. Dad said he was sure I would get that chance at some point because he had invited Jesus and his disciples to stay in our house when he came to Jerusalem. "How many disciples?" was mother's first question. "Seemed like about ten or twelve," father said. "But don't worry, we have the room and the staff to make them comfortable."

Interviewer: I assume they did come at some point. Can you tell us about the first time Jesus and his disciples stayed at your house?

Mark: It was at the time of the Passover. Father had alerted me to be aware that Jesus might come to stay, and to be ready to welcome him. About a week before the Passover, I was in the front of the house when two unfamiliar men came up and began to untie our donkey. When they saw me, they told me that their master had sent them and that he needed to borrow the animal for the day. They promised to return it when he was through with it. "Who is your master?" I boldly asked. "Our master is the teacher, Jesus."

"Yes, yes," I said, "My father knows your Master and has instructed me to do whatever you need to make him comfortable in our home. Please, take the donkey."

I immediately ran into the house yelling, "He's here!" "Who is here?" Rhoda said. "Jesus. Jesus and his friends," I said, "and father has invited them to stay here." Rhoda, who was our maid ran off frantically mumbling something about wishing she had more warning that there would be guests.

It was late that evening when one of Jesus' friends arrived at the door and knocked. He was there to return the donkey and to let us know that Jesus would be staying with friends in Bethany the next couple of nights, but that he would very much appreciate it if they could join us for the Passover feast later in the week.

They had apparently had a busy day. I heard them talking about coming into the city from the Mount of Olives and people waving tree branches and shouting for Jesus to be made king. It sounded like a grand procession and I would have loved to have been there! Then they talked about going to the temple and how upset Jesus had been when he saw all the buying and selling of animals and souvenirs going on in the temple courtyard. Father nodded in agreement since that was something that he always felt was inappropriate if not downright sacrilegious.

A couple of days later, I convinced Father to take me to the temple so we could listen to Jesus teach. The temple courtyard was mobbed with people who had come for the grand Passover celebration. As usual, there were a lot of teachers spread around the courtyard. Each one had his gathering of students or listeners around him. It wasn't hard to find Jesus in all the commotion because the crowd around him was three times larger than any of the others.

While we were listening, some of the Pharisees asked him a question about paying taxes to the Romans. "Does the Law of Moses allow people to pay taxes to Caesar or not?" they asked. There was something in the way they asked the question that made me think they had another purpose in mind other than asking just to get an answer.

Apparently Jesus sensed the same treachery in their voices. He told them to show him a coin and asked them, "Whose picture is on the coin?" "Caesar's," they replied.

"Then give to Caesar what belongs to Caesar. But give to God what belongs to God," Jesus answered.

I immediately thought about the passage from the Book of the Psalms that says, "Know that the Lord is God. He made us; we belong to him." Jesus had answered their question without giving them what they wanted. Ooh! They were so angry!

There were also some Sadducees trying to question him. When they got the chance, they outlined a lengthy old rabbinical riddle that we struggled with in school. They said a man with seven brothers dies and each of his brothers, in turn, marries his widow after the one before died. This was what the law instructed. Their question was when the woman who had been married to all eight brothers dies, whose wife will she be in heaven?

Everyone who heard their question knew they weren't being serious because Sadducees don't really believe in resurrection. Jesus chided them for not knowing the scripture or having any idea about God's power. What he said was that there won't be any marriage in heaven, but that we will be like God's angels. As for resurrection, he lifted up the words of God to Moses at the burning bush when God said, "I am the God of life, not death."

Later on when all the Scribes and Pharisees and Sadducees had cleared away, there was one young student of the law who stayed on to listen to the Teacher. When Jesus asked him, "Young man, do you have a question?" the young lawyer asked, timidly, "Which commandment is the most important of all?" Knowing that this question was a genuine question from the man's heart, Jesus didn't play around with his answer as he did sometimes when he answered the Pharisees and Sadducees.

Jesus replied "The most important one is 'Israel, listen! Our God is the one Lord, and you must love the Lord your God with all your heart, with all your being, with all your mind, and with all your strength.'" Then he quickly added, "You must love your neighbor as yourself." No other commandment is greater than these."

The young lawyer said, "I agree with you Teacher, when you say that our God is one and to love God with all of the heart, with a full understanding, and all of one's strength, and to love one's neighbor as oneself are much greater commandments than what kind of offering gets burned on the altar. Jesus told him, "You aren't far from God's kingdom, young man."

Interviewer: Can you tell us about the Passover feast? Who was there? What was it like having Jesus in the house with your family?"

Mark: When the day of Passover came, one of my father's servants had gone to the community well to draw water. On his way home, he noticed two men following him. When he got to the gate, he called for my father to come speak to the men. The two men said they were asking on behalf of their master, Jesus, if the room for the Passover was ready for them to come. After looking at the room we had over the main house, the two men left to tell Jesus that all was ready.

That evening Jesus arrived with his twelve disciples and a few others. When he saw me, he put his hand on my head and said, "I saw you in the temple the other day, didn't I?" "Yes, sir," I said, and offered to take his cloak.

When the sun had set, we all gathered at the table. And by "all" I mean my parents, several aunts and uncles and cousins, Jesus and his twelve and some of their family members. There were people who I thought were his servants, but it turns out they were just people who had heard him teach and believed the truth of what he was teaching about love and forgiveness and how it is better to serve others than to have others serve you. There was quite a crowd in that upstairs room. Rhoda was frantic!

During the supper, Jesus said, out of nowhere, "I assure you, one of you eating with me will betray me." We all wondered who he might be talking about. We assumed it couldn't be one of his disciples, but who? People began asking him, "Is it I, Lord?" But Jesus answered, "It is one of the twelve who is dipping bread with me into this bowl." He said, "The Son of Man will go to his death just as it is written. But how terrible it will be for that one who betrays him! It would be better for him if he had never been born."

Shortly thereafter, one of them got up and left hurriedly. I can't tell you which one it was since I didn't know all their names yet.

Then came the time in the meal to raise up the unleavened bread and remind the children that it is eaten to serve as a reminder of the flat bread the Jews had when they escaped Egypt so quickly. But, as Jesus held up the bread that night and blessed it and broke it, he said, "From now on I want this bread to remind you of my body which will soon be broken for you."

When he took the cup of wine which served as a reminder of the blood of the sacrificed lamb whose blood was spread on the doorposts of the Hebrew homes in Egypt so the angel of death would "Passover" them, he said, "I am the lamb of God. I am to be sacrificed for the sins of all the world, not just the children of Israel. Take this cup to remember the new covenant I am making with you – the covenant of love and forgiveness." I don't think any of us will ever forget that moment!

After some good, lively singing, Jesus and the twelve took their leave and said they were going out to pray. I know some people don't believe what I am going to tell you now, but it is true.

I was able to sneak away from the house and follow them. They went to a place on the side of the Mount of Olives facing the wall of the city and the temple. It was an old olive grove called Gethsemane, which means "oil press." I stayed back a little not wanting to get caught and not wanting to be a bother. I could see the men all get comfortable under the trees while Jesus and three of them walked away from the group a little. It was dark and cold, and I was tired after the whole day of preparations and celebrations. I fell asleep.

I don't know how long it was, but I was awakened by the sounds of a lot of men approaching. They weren't even trying to be quiet! They were guards from the temple as far as I could see in the dark. They stopped just short

of reaching the group of men when one of their number
stepped forward. I'm not sure, but he looked like the one
who had left the dinner when Jesus said one of them
would betray him. He seemed to be looking for someone
in particular when Jesus came back from where he had
been praying. When the man saw him, he went up to
him and gave him the customary kiss of hospitality on
his cheek. As soon as he did, the guard moved in and
surrounded Jesus and put him into shackles.

A scuffle broke out as the rest of us tried to get away.
I was almost caught when one of the soldiers grabbed my
tunic. I managed to slip out of my clothes and ran off
naked! I knew I would be in trouble when I got home
for having left without permission and for coming back
without my clothes. But before anyone could yell at me,
I found an old towel to wrap around me and I began to
tell them that Jesus had been arrested. I told them about
the soldiers, the kiss, the shackles, the scuffle – all of it.

Not long after I got back to the house, his disciples
started showing up one or two at a time. They begged my
father to let them in since they had nowhere else to go.
Of course they were let in and taken back to the upper
room where we had just had supper. My father said they
could stay as long as they needed. The big one, the one
named Peter, said he was going to go out and try to find
out where they had taken Jesus.

It was a long tense night as we awaited word from
Peter. At dawn, just after the rooster crowed, Peter
returned back to the house. He had been crying. Through
his sobs he told us that they had taken Jesus to the home

of the high priest and then to the court of the Roman governor, Pilate. Because we were afraid that Pilate might send soldiers to look for Jesus' followers, we all stayed behind the locked gates of the house. Later, when it was suggested that we send someone out to find out what was happening, I quickly volunteered. I said, "I am just a boy (actually, I had already had my Bar Mitzvah.) I said they won't be looking for a boy!" To my surprise, my father agreed to let me go out. Before he could say it, I said, "Don't worry, Father, I'll be careful."

When I got close to the temple area, it wasn't hard to figure out what was happening. The soldiers were leading a loud and angry crowd toward the gate on the north side of the city. I could hear people cheering, "Crucify him!" When I got a glimpse of their prisoner, it was Jesus. He was bloody and had the bloody beam of a Roman cross laid across his back. He kept falling from the load and whenever he did, the soldiers seemed to take pleasure in whipping him until he got up. At one point when Jesus could no longer get up, they grabbed a man out of the crowd and forced him to carry the beam.

It was obvious they were headed to "the place of the skull" as that little hill where they often crucified prisoners was called. I turned and ran back home as fast as I could and told the others. A shudder of fear went up from everyone in the room. Without saying anything, some of the women in the group immediately left the room to make sure they would be there if he needed anything and to learn where they might take his body after he was dead.

They were exhausted when they returned late that night, but they said they knew where the grave was. They told us some of the things Jesus had said while on the cross. They said that at one point Jesus cried out that he felt forsaken by God. But the thing I will remember as long as I live is what he said about those who were tormenting him. He said, "Father, forgive them. They don't know what they are doing."

The morning following the Sabbath, before I woke up, some of the women had already left to go to the tomb to prepare Jesus' body for burial. Just after daybreak, though, they came running back and were almost hysterical as they told us that the tomb was empty and they had not seen Jesus' body! Instead they saw an angel who told them that Jesus had been raised up from the dead! That he wasn't there! And then the angel let them look into the tomb and sure enough, it was empty! Not fully believing what the women were reporting, Peter and John ran to the tomb to see for themselves. When they returned they verified the report of the women, but they were visibly troubled.

That same day, in the evening, the disciples were all in the room alone and talking about what to do next. Suddenly, Jesus was there with them! He said they touched his wounds and saw him eat a piece of bread. He told them to wait in Jerusalem until they received instructions from God, and that in the meantime, God would be with them in spirit.

During the next month we saw Jesus several more times. Other people in other places were apparently seeing him as well. One day, hundreds of people were praying together when Jesus appeared to them. More and more people found our house and joined the fellowship of Jesus' followers. The disciples went with Jesus one day to a hilltop near Bethany where he told them to stay in Jerusalem until they received God's Spirit. They said they watched as he was "taken up to heaven in a cloud."

In the days that followed, his friends continued to use our home as a gathering place. As more and more people joined the group, it became more like a movement -- a movement to spread the wonderful news of all the things Jesus had said and promised. On the festival of Weeks, there must have been more than a hundred friends of Jesus gathered upstairs at the house with hundreds more outside. While Peter was leading them in prayers, the gentle breeze suddenly turned into a blast of wind. It blew the shutters of the room open! I'm not sure I can adequately describe to you what happened next.

Interviewer: Oh, please try! Please tell us what you saw.

Mark: The people in the room began talking in all the different languages of the world. Those outside began to recognize their own language as they heard it, and soon they were saying that the people inside must be drunk! Peter stepped to the window and silenced the crowd with his booming voice. He said, "These people are not drunk! It's only 9:00 in the morning! They are overcome by the Spirit of God!" He went on to preach to them about what the prophets had said, and about who Jesus was. It was the first time I heard anyone say that Jesus was the Christ, the Messiah chosen and sent by God to save the world.

Peter kept preaching and when he finished, 3,000 or more people wanted to join our fellowship of believers. The more the fellowship grew, the more it seemed that the authorities tried to stop it. They began arresting the leaders, John and Peter, and others. They were warning them to stop teaching about Jesus, and when they didn't, they put them in the jail.

One night after Peter had been arrested, he told us an angel appeared to him and led him out of the jail. He made his way through the dark streets back to our house. But when he knocked on the door, Rhoda saw him and in her excitement and confusion she slammed the door on him as she ran to tell Father. Eventually we figured out what that hysterical woman was saying and we went to the door and let Peter in, out of the danger of the streets.

The church, as we came to be called, grew and grew as more people heard the word and eagerly believed in the loving God that Jesus had spoken of. Soon there were small groups of believers meeting in other homes, and not only in Jerusalem. Even when the authorities started arresting our members, people continued to come to us. Anyway, that is the way it was in the beginning.

Interviewer: Is there anything else you would like to say?

Mark: There is so much more that I can tell you. Many years later, I had the opportunity to travel with my cousin Barnabas and Paul. I spent time as a prisoner with Paul and Peter in Rome. After Paul's execution, I stayed with Peter and wrote down as much of what he told me as I could.

Let me just finish by saying that the way I saw Jesus treat the people he met, the sick and outcast, the rich and the needy, and the way he treated me when I was so young showed me that choosing to love other people rather than envying them or judging or fighting them is a much more peaceful way to journey through this life.

Just remember what I heard Jesus say at that Passover meal: "Don't be troubled or afraid. You will never be alone. God will send his own Spirit to be with you forever and to give you peace."

Interviewer: Thank you so much, Mark.

Chapter 8

Thomas, the twin
John 11:11-16

IN THIS CHAPTER, WE ARE going to be interviewing another of "The Twelve" of Jesus' disciples. Thomas is mentioned in all four gospels and the Book of Acts; however, it is only in the Gospel of John that we hear more about Thomas than just finding his name in the lists of the disciples. We hear Thomas speak in John 11:16 after the death of Lazarus; in John 14:5 in the upper room; and in John 20:24 following the resurrection.

Interviewer: Sir, before I ask you about these three moments in your time with Jesus, I really would like for you to clarify some little confusion that exists about your name. The writer of John repeatedly calls you "Thomas, the twin." You are also called "Didymus" at times. Can you explain?

Thomas: The name "Thomas" is really your English version of the Aramaic word *Te'oma* which means "twin."

The Greek word for "twin" is *Didymus*. So, no matter which language you use, my name means "twin."

Interviewer: There is also some speculation that you were Jesus' twin brother. Is that true?

Thomas: And others say that I had a twin brother. But if you think about the Christmas story that you know so well, there is no mention of Mary giving birth to twins. As for a twin brother, some say I had a twin brother who died at birth and that is why I was named "the twin." Others just said I looked like Jesus.

Interviewer: The first time you are mentioned in John's gospel is at the time of the death of Lazarus, Jesus' friend. What can you tell us about those days?

Thomas: Jesus had often talked about a friend he had in the small town of Bethany, near Jerusalem. His friend's name was Lazarus. Apparently Lazarus was not a well person. Lazarus had two sisters who took care of him and kept Jesus informed of his condition. One day we received word from the sisters, Mary and Martha, that was much more urgent than usual. They said that their brother, whom Jesus loved very much, was gravely ill. They pleaded with Jesus to come quickly and minister to Lazarus.

When Jesus didn't immediately make preparations to go to Bethany to help Lazarus, we all asked why? Jesus said that Lazarus' illness wasn't going to end in his death. He said that the illness was for the "glory of God and that

God's Son would be glorified through it." Two days later Jesus said, "It is time, now, for us to go to Bethany."

We had all decided that Jesus' hesitancy in going to Bethany was due to the order that had been issued for his arrest. One of the men said, "Rabbi, the Jewish opposition wants to stone you, why would you want to go back?"

Jesus responded in a way we didn't understand at first. He said, "Our friend Lazarus is sleeping, but I am going to wake him up." Someone said, "Lord, if he's just sleeping, he will get well, why risk it." We didn't understand that Jesus was saying that Lazarus was dead.

Jesus then told us plainly, "Lazarus has died. For your sakes, I'm glad I wasn't there so that you can believe. Now let's go to him."

I listened as the others tried to get Jesus to change his mind and not go because of the possible danger we would encounter there. So I said, "Look, if it is Jesus' intention to go to Bethany, then let us all go with Jesus and let us be prepared to die with him if it comes to that!"

When we arrived we were told that Lazarus had already been in the tomb for four days. Quite a large gathering of friends of the family had already gathered in Bethany (which is only two miles from Jerusalem.)

Someone ran to the house to tell the sisters that Jesus had finally arrived. Martha came running out to meet us and threw herself at the feet of Jesus. Through her tears she said, "Lord, I know that if you had only been here, our brother would not have died. But I still believe that whatever you ask of God, God will give you."

What Jesus said next was startling. He said, "Martha, your brother will rise again." Martha said, "Yes Lord, I know that he will rise in the resurrection on the last day."

Jesus then said to her, "Martha, I am the resurrection and the life. Whoever believes in me will live, even though they die. In fact, everyone who lives and believes in me will never die. Do you believe this?"

Martha replied, "Yes, Lord, I believe that you are the Christ, God's Son, sent into the world."

It took me a while to sort through what Jesus was saying. The best I could figure is that he was saying that even though my body will die, as all of our bodies will die, we will still have life and that if we will live in these bodies believing in Jesus as God's Son and heed to his words, we will never be without life – whether in this body or not.

After saying those things, Martha excused herself to go and tell Mary that Jesus was there. Mary quickly got up and left the mourners at the house and ran to Jesus. She fell at his feet as her sister had done and said basically the same thing her sister had said, "Lord, if you only had been here, our brother wouldn't have died." Mary was crying so grievously, as were the other mourners that Jesus didn't even try to be heard over the wailing. He simply asked to be taken to the tomb where they had buried Lazarus.

Jesus himself was moved to tears as he stood outside the tomb of his beloved friend. Then Jesus said to some of the men who were there, "Remove the stone." Martha said, "But Lord, it has been four days that the body has been in the tomb. The smell will be awful!"

Jesus said, "Didn't I tell you that if you believe, you will see God's glory?" So they removed the stone. Jesus looked up and prayed, "Father, thank you for hearing me. I know you always hear me. I am asking this for the benefit of the crowd standing here so that they will believe that you sent me." Having said that, Jesus shouted with a loud voice as if calling to someone far away, "Lazarus, come out!" We all focused on the entrance of the tomb! Nothing happened for a long time, but then, deep in the darkness of that grave we could see a figure moving and before long, still bound in his grave cloths, Lazarus stepped into the light. Jesus simply said to them, as though what was happening was as normal as the sunrise, "Untie him and let him go."

Lazarus was terribly weak, as you can imagine, but with some help he was able to walk back to the house where he was given something to eat. We stayed and visited for a while, but then, so Lazarus could get some rest, we left. As we were walking, I asked Jesus, "How were you so certain that the soldiers wouldn't arrest you?" Jesus said, "God will determine the time for those things to happen, not sinful men."

We soon learned that the chief priests and Pharisees had become very afraid of the popularity Jesus had among the Jewish people, and that they were determined to have him killed, one way or another!

Even though it was getting close to time for the Passover feast, Jesus decided it would be better for us to retreat to the hill country of Ephraim north of Jerusalem. A friend reported to us that the priests and Pharisees had given orders that anyone who knew where Jesus was should report it so they could arrest him.

Interviewer: We know you were all in Jerusalem for that Passover. Please tell us about those days.

Thomas: Well, as you know, there was quite a scene as we entered the city. Jesus was riding a donkey and the crowds were cheering his name. We went to the home of a believer who had a room upstairs where we could have the feast.

When we arrived, our host family had everything ready and made sure to seat Jesus in the seat of honor. Their servants were busy moving around serving the meal and filling the cups. By the way they treated him, they had obviously been told that Jesus was the guest of honor. But Jesus would have none of that kind of treatment. Shortly, he got up and found a basin of water and a towel and began to move around the table washing every one's feet. When he got to Peter, Peter recoiled and refused to allow Jesus to wash his feet. "No Lord! Not mine!" he declared.

Jesus looked at Peter and said, "You don't understand what I am doing now, but soon you will." Peter said, "Lord, you will never wash my stinking feet!" Jesus replied, "Peter, unless I wash you, you won't have a place with me."

Then Peter said, "Then Lord, you need to wash all of me for I am filthy from head to toe." Jesus said, "Peter, you are not as dirty as you think. I have seen you do good things and I know you have a good heart. But like the others, you are not completely clean." Jesus proceeded to wash Peter's feet.

After he had washed the feet of each of us, he returned to his place at the table and asked us, "Do you know what I've done for you? You call me 'Teacher' and 'Lord', and you are right, because I am. If I, your Lord and teacher, have washed your feet, you too must wash each other's feet. I have given you an example: just as I have done, you also must do. I assure you, servants aren't greater than their master, nor are those who are sent greater than the one who sent them. Since you know these things, you will be happy if you do them.'"

Then he said something about someone who was going to betray him. We all asked who it was, but he only said something about it being one of us at the table. Judas got up and left the room about that time, but, at the time, I didn't connect that with Jesus' words about a betrayer.

Then Jesus talked again about his desire that we love each other, as he had often said. He said, "There is really only one thing that I command you to do in my name. Love each other just as I have loved you." He said, "This is how everyone will know that you are my disciples, when you love each other."

Then the conversation got a little strange. He said that he would only be with us for a little longer and then he would go someplace where we could not go. Peter said, "Lord, where are you going?"

Jesus answered, "Where I am going, you can't follow me now, but you will follow later." Peter protested and said he was ready to give up his life for Jesus.

Then Jesus told all of us, "Don't be troubled. Trust in God. Trust also in me." He said, "My Father's house has rooms to spare. I am going to prepare a room for each of you. And I will come back and take you to be with me in my Father's house. You know the way to the place I'm going."

I thought about those words for a second and being the realistic person I am, I said, "Lord, we don't know where you are going. How can we possibly know the way?"

When Jesus replied, "Thomas, I am the way." I didn't have to think long before I realized that what he was saying was that the way he had lived his life was the way we should live if we wanted to follow him.

I thought about the other ways people lived – the Romans relying on their military; the Greeks with their deep, confusing philosophical writings; the Babylonians and Persians with their long lists of gods; and the heathen who did nothing to help anyone but themselves. When I compared those "ways" of living with the way of Jesus, I knew right away that his way was the way I wanted to follow.

Then he added, "I am also the truth." I immediately thought back to the words of the Psalmist who said, "Make your ways known to me, Lord; teach me your paths. Lead me in your truth. Teach it to me – because you are the God who saves me." Jesus is the truth that we need to learn. Jesus is the truth of what God is. God is loving, forgiving, welcoming, and healing. Jesus is loving, forgiving, welcoming, and healing. God is like what Jesus is. In fact, Jesus added, "If you have really known me, you also know the Father."

Philip then said what we were all thinking, "Lord, show us the Father and that will be enough for us."

Jesus then said, very plainly, "Whoever has seen me has seen the Father. I am in the Father and the Father is in me. The words I have spoken are the words of the Father that are in me. The works I have done are the works the Father has me do. I assure you," he said, "that whoever believes in me will do the works that I do. They will do even greater works than these because I am going to the Father."

He then promised us that when he was gone to the Father, we would not be alone. He said that God would be with us in his Holy Spirit and he would continue to teach us and guide us and walk with us.

One of the final things he said before we left the room was, "I want to leave you with peace – my peace which is not like what the world thinks of as peace." I knew exactly what he was talking about. You see, the Romans kept talking about "the Peace of Rome" by which they meant that if we did what we were told by our oppressors, there would be peace (meaning they wouldn't kill us!) Jesus was talking about the peace that comes when we have nothing left to worry about – especially not death. He said, "Don't be troubled and don't be afraid. The Father will be with you, always, in Spirit."

Interviewer: Before we let you go, can you tell us about what happened on the day of Christ's resurrection?

Thomas: We were all huddled in that upstairs room where we had eaten the Passover feast when suddenly the women who had gone to the tomb to wash and prepare Jesus' body for its final burial came running into the room. They were shouting, "He is not there! He is not there!"

"What are you talking about?" we all asked. "When we got to the tomb, the big stone was rolled aside and there was no body in the tomb!" they said. "Did you go into the tomb?" someone asked. They said, "No, we just looked inside. Then we heard someone behind us, and thinking it might be the guard, we turned in fear. But it was the gardener, we thought. The man said, "The one you are looking for is not here. He has risen!"'

We all thought they must be delusional. Someone said, "They didn't actually go into the grave. Maybe they missed seeing the body." Peter said that he would go and double check. John agreed to go with him. The rest of us waited in the safety of the upper room. We questioned the women over and over, but their story never changed.

After about an hour, Peter and John returned. They told us that John had outrun Peter and when he got to the tomb, he knelt down outside and was looking in when Peter arrived and went straight into the tomb. He said that when his eyes adjusted to the darkness, he could tell that there was no body there. He said that the grave cloths that had been wrapped around his body were neatly folded and lying on the stone. He said the cloth that had been placed over his face was also folded and lying at the other end. Then John also went in and saw the same thing.

Mary from Magdala had also gone to the tomb and arrived just as Peter and John were leaving. When she looked into the tomb, she said she saw two angels in white, sitting where the body should have been. She said the angels asked her why she was crying. She told them she thought someone had stolen the body of her Lord and she wanted to find him. She said she turned to go, and as soon as she did, there was the man that looked like he could be the gardener as the women had reported.

She said she asked the man if he knew where the body of Jesus was. The man simply said, "Mary." She immediately recognized his voice and cried, "Teacher!" She said that Jesus wouldn't let her touch him, but told her to come back and tell the rest of us that she had seen him.

We didn't know what to think. How could it be true? Someone remembered Jesus saying something about returning. I remembered Jesus saying that he would rise in three days, but I never thought he meant like this. As a pall settled over the room and each one became quiet and reflective, I decided to go for a walk.

I walked back along the route we had taken to the Mt. of Olives and the Garden of Gethsemane where Jesus had been betrayed and arrested. I found the spot where Jesus had kneeled and I knelt there and prayed. I lost track of time and when I finally made my way back, most of the group was asleep, but there were a few who were awake and greeted me with the most unbelievable news. "He was here!" they said, "Jesus was here! He showed us his wounds and said, "Peace be upon you. As the Father sent me, so I am sending you." Then he said for us to receive the Holy Spirit and that if we forgive anyone's sins, they will surely be forgiven by the Father.

I so wanted to believe all they were telling me, but I knew that unless I could see for myself the wounds from the nails and the crown of thorns and the whip on his back that I would always have doubts. Nothing like what they were saying had ever happened before. How could I believe without seeing?

All week I listened as they told each other and others what they had seen. And all week I felt a kind of emptiness in my heart. The kind of emptiness you feel when you want something to be true, but you have no way of being sure.

On the following Sunday we were all again in the upper room sharing a meal when, suddenly, Jesus was there with us. He came over to where I was sitting and held out his hands for me to see the wounds, and invited me to touch the wound from the spear in his side. He said, "Thomas, there is no longer any reason for you to have doubts. Believe, Thomas."

I fell to the floor and cried out, "My Lord and my God!"

Jesus said, "It is good that you have come to believe because you have seen. But happy also are those who are able to believe without having seen." There is so much more that Jesus did in the weeks he stayed with us before returning to the Father.

Interviewer: We don't hear anything about your life as the church got going. Could you tell us what you were doing and what your life was like after that?

Thomas: I went east. First I went into Syria to preach, and then I followed the line of Jewish settlements along the Spice Road through what you know as Iran, Iraq, Afghanistan, and Pakistan and then down into India along the Malabar Coast. Along the way, I occasionally met small groups of Jesus' followers who had heard the good news from some who had been in Jerusalem on that day of Pentecost when the Holy Spirit had filled us with the power to speak in so many languages.

I arrived in India about 20 years after the resurrection of our Lord and was able to organize many congregations of believers before I was martyred with a spear. To this day, there are 28 million "Thomas Christians", as they are known, in India. That's about 3% of the population.

The first president of India, Rajendra Prasad, speaking at a Thomas celebration in New Delhi in 1955, said, "Saint Thomas came to India when many of the countries of Europe had not yet become Christian, and so these Indians who trace their Christianity to him have a longer and higher ancestry than that of Christians of many European countries. It is a matter of pride to us that it so happened."

There are still seven churches in India that sprang forth from my ministry. I won't try to tell you their names because they are impossible to pronounce. But if you would like to see pictures of them, go to the internet and search for "History of Christianity in India: Seven Churches established by St. Thomas in Kerala, India."

So, if you want to visit one of the oldest fellowships of gathered Christians in the world, welcome to India!

Chapter 9

Nicodemus, a Pharisee

John 3:1-18

IN THIS CHAPTER WE ARE interviewing a person about whom we have no personal information but his name. However, this individual was a participant in one of the most important and widely known conversations with Jesus in any of the gospels. Our guest today is Nicodemus. Nicodemus was a Pharisee and is mentioned on three separate occasions in the Gospel of John.

Interviewer: Good morning, sir.

Nicodemus: Good morning.

Interviewer: Sir, we know nothing about you except that you were a Pharisee who came to Jesus at night. But before we get into the conversation you shared with Jesus, I think it is important for our audience to understand just what a "Pharisee" was. Most of the references we have in the gospels paint the Pharisees in a negative light. Most of the time they are challenging Jesus with the intent of finding something to accuse him of. Please tell us just what it meant to be a Pharisee.

Nicodemus: That's a good question. Let me illustrate by asking you what political party you are a member of? Most of you are not actually "a member" of your party – you simply identify with one party or the other. Likely, the only document you have that indicates which party you identify with is the voter registration card in your wallet. So does that make you a member of the party? Do you pay dues, attend meetings? Likely not. But there are certain attitudes or principles of one party that you agree with more than the other. That is what makes you a Democrat or a Republican. Being a Pharisee was a lot like that. We weren't an organization. We didn't wear a uniform. We didn't recite a binding pledge. Basically, a Pharisee was a man who called himself a Pharisee, or whom others called a Pharisee. We held certain principles about our faith and we tried to live by them.

Interviewer: Can you tell us what were some of the identifiable ideas of the Pharisees and where did they originate?

Nicodemus: Well, you may have noticed that there were no Pharisees mentioned in the Old Testament. The beginning of the Pharisees was in the time of the great Maccabean conflict about 150 years before the time when Jesus and I lived.

Interviewer: I'm afraid most of us don't know very much about that time either. Could you refresh our memories?

Nicodemus: Let me try. Alexander the Greek came through our land about 300 years before Christ. When he moved on to India, he left his generals in charge of Palestine. For the next 200 years the Greek culture was imported onto our land and people. That time, known as the time of "Hellenization", almost destroyed the faithfulness of the Jews to our ancient ways of worship and the honoring of the God of our Fathers. People became more accustomed to hearing about the Greek gods, and some even became comfortable leaving offerings at their altars.

As I said, about 150 years before the time of Jesus, we Jews revolted against the intrusion of Greek ways into our very traditional society. Those who resisted the Greek ways and tried to separate from that influence and preserve the traditional ways of our faith were called "Separatists", which is what the word "Pharisee" means.

The Pharisees were all about faithfully maintaining the study of our prophets and history and living those teachings in our lives. We emphasized the necessity of worship at the Temple and the observance of our rich law code. Pharisees believed that obedience to the law was what God wanted and was equivalent to obedience to God's will and would lead to salvation for our nation.

When the Roman General Pompey moved the Greeks out and established Roman authority over our nation, the Pharisees continued to lead the movement for separation from the pagan religious practices of the Romans. We were called to be a holy people and a kingdom of priests, and that meant that we must live according to the ancient laws.

As you might imagine, some Pharisees were more radical in their opposition to the Romans, while others were willing to compromise in order to maintain our national identity. But for all of us, it was a treacherous path we were walking – we never could be sure what small thing would make the Romans angry and set into motion a crackdown against our people. While we continued to be the "separatists" -- the "Pharisees" – demanding compliance to the traditions of the Jews, we also had to advise caution and sometimes even compliance with the demands of our oppressors. That's why Jesus presented such a dilemma for us.

Interviewer: How was that?

Nicodemus: Before I ever heard of Jesus, I went with some other Pharisees out to the river where there were reports of a crazy man preaching about the "judgment that was coming soon." The man began railing against Pharisees and Sadducees saying that we needed to "produce fruit that would show that our hearts and lives were changed." He said that just because we were confident that we were children of Abraham, that wouldn't be enough. He said God could raise up children of Abraham from the rocks in the river!

That man's message caught my attention. For a long time, I had felt that just going through the motions of sacrifices and offerings and strictly obeying the law wasn't enough. It didn't make me feel like I was very holy.

At first we weren't sure where Jesus stood in terms of the law and traditions of the Jews. For example, Jesus was fond of saying that he had not come to get rid of the Law and the Prophets. He even said that the law and prophets would not pass away as long as earth and heaven exists. He said that someone who ignores the law and teaches others to do the same will be lowly regarded in the coming kingdom, while those who keep the law will be elevated in the kingdom of heaven. All that was acceptable to us Pharisees. It sounded like he was holding up the Pharisees for compliment. After all, that's what we did. We kept the law and taught others to do the same.

But then he said that what he really came to do was to fulfill the law. He told the crowds that unless they showed a righteousness greater than that of us Pharisees, they stood no chance of entering the kingdom of heaven.

What? What did that mean?

He then talked about specific laws. He said, "The law says not to murder or you will be liable for your actions on the judgment day." Now that is clear enough, right? But then he said, "But I say that whoever is angry with his brother or sister will not do well on the judgment day." Well, we all get angry, don't we? What did he mean? It sounded like he was saying that just obeying the law was not enough.

He said, "The law says you shall not commit adultery. But I say that every man who looks at a woman with lust in his eyes, has already committed adultery in his heart." What's wrong with the way the law said it?

He said the old law of limiting your retaliation against someone who has harmed you is not good enough. He said, "An eye for an eye or a tooth for a tooth" is not good enough. He said we shouldn't oppose someone who is out to harm us. He said if your enemy slaps you, you should turn and let him slap you on your other cheek as well. In the same way, if they sue you for your coat, give them your shirt as well. If you are ordered to carry a soldier's burden for a mile, keep going until you have carried it two miles. (Matthew 5:38-42) Who thinks like that?

And then he said the most preposterous thing I think I have ever heard. He said, "The law says you must love your neighbor and hate your enemy. But I say to you, love your enemies and pray for those who harass you and do good to those who persecute you." I mean really? The law gives very clear guidance as to how to retaliate against our enemies and it says nothing about letting them get away with their treachery.

He said that when God in heaven makes it rain, the rain falls on the fields of the good person as well as the evil man. I had never thought of that! And when the sun shines it shines on both the righteous person and the unrighteous. He said that if we will do good to those who do evil to us, then we will be like children of God.

I began to see what he was getting at. As long as we were satisfied with just obeying laws and commandments, we were not thinking about the impact we were having on other people. In fact, we could go about making sure we were not doing anything against the law and never even think about how our actions were affecting other people. We had, it seemed, made our religion to be just about gaining God's favor for me. No one else mattered.

Interviewer: Now, about that nighttime meeting you had with Jesus that John reports about in his gospel. Why did you go to him in the dark?

Nicodemus: Well, you see, quite a split was developing among many of the Pharisees. There were those who believed that Jesus was just pretending to keep the law while he was actually telling people they could ignore it. A much smaller group of us felt like Jesus had something important to teach us.

It seemed to me that he was not telling us to disobey the law, but that the law itself was just a tool to help us achieve the higher righteousness of loving neighbors.

I wanted to know more. I tried to think of a way to get close to Jesus without drawing attention to myself. I knew that there were Pharisees who, if they found out, would attack me for not being committed to the preservation of the old law and the way it had always been interpreted. I knew there were always eyes watching, whether they were Romans or spies of the high priest who was answerable to the Romans. Besides, Jesus was always surrounded by his disciples and a large crowd.

I decided to go at night when at least I had a chance of not being noticed though I knew that I would have to announce myself to Jesus' disciples before I could talk to him.

When I found myself standing in front of Jesus, I suddenly lost my train of thought. I said something about knowing that he was a teacher sent by God. I said, "No one could do the things you have done unless the Spirit of God was with him."

Jesus just looked at me for a minute. It felt like he was not looking at the Nicodemus everyone else saw when they looked at me. It felt as though he was looking into me, into my soul. Then, with no regard to whatever feeble thing I had just said, he answered the question that I had not been able to ask.

He said, "Nicodemus, unless you are born from above you will not see God's kingdom." "What?" I stammered. He repeated, "Unless a person is born over again, he will not be included in God's kingdom."

"But how can I be born again?" I asked. "How can a person reenter his mother's womb and be born again? That's impossible!"

Jesus said, "Nicodemus, your physical birth gave you all the things you need to function in the physical world – strength to work, mental ability to figure things out, fear to flee from danger, reasoning to solve problems, eyes for seeing and ears for hearing. But you also need to be able to function in a spiritual world – a world of unseen realities like faith and hope and love. You need ears that can hear the call of God. You need eyes that can see the way God works. You need the sensitivity to empathize with the needs of others and the courage to respond to their needs with no concern for what that response will cost you."

Jesus continued saying that in the physical world into which we were all born, we are constantly trying to be in control. We try to control all the things that happen to us. We want to know what has happened, why it happened, and how we can deal with what happened. But there is more to life than just what we can see and control. There are realities in life that can't be seen but are just as true as those that can.

There is a spiritual reality to life. There is love and hope and fear. There is wonder and sorrow. There is God. God's spirit is like the wind that blows wherever it wishes. You hear its sound, but you don't know where it comes from or where it is going. You can't control it no matter how you try. You must be born into that spirit world just as you were born into this physical one. You must learn to let that Spirit control you.

"But how?" I asked Jesus.

Jesus said, "You are a teacher of Israel, how is it that you don't know what I am telling you?"

I said, "I teach the law and the law can be seen. It is written down. And I can see the effects of the law when it is kept or when it is broken. The law gives security and structure to our communities. The law provides stability in our nation. We keep the law because the law is God's law and above all else, keeping the law is what God wants from us. When the law is not observed, God becomes angry and lashes out at us."

Jesus said, "Nicodemus, you wanted to ask me how a person could see the kingdom of heaven. You have witnessed the things I have done in this world.

You have seen those who were fed and healed. You have witnessed the joy a child feels when I have taken time to stop what I was doing and give that child a moment of attention and love. You have likely heard about the time I spent in Samaria befriending those good people – your enemies. The things I have done in this world were done so that you could understand the way it is with God. If you don't understand the things I have done in this world, how will you be able to understand if I tell you about the things that are done in God's kingdom?"

Jesus went on to say that no one has ever gone to heaven and then come back to tell what he saw, but, he said, he had come to us from heaven and he must be "raised up" just like Moses lifted up the serpent in the wilderness as a sign of God's power and presence with Moses and the people.

Interviewer: That saying about raising up the serpent has always seemed a strange thing for Jesus to say in that moment. Could you shed some light on what he meant?

Nicodemus: You see, when our people were in the desert with Moses leading them, they fought many battles and the Lord God gave them victory. But on one occasion, after they had defeated the Canaanites, rather than giving thanks, they began complaining about not having enough food or water, and about the miserable bread. So, the Lord sent poisonous snakes among them. Some were bitten and died! They complained to Moses.

Moses prayed to the Lord for the people. That's when God said to Moses, "Make a poisonous snake out of bronze and lift it up on a tall pole so all could see it. Whoever is bitten by one of the real snakes and then looks at the bronze snake that is lifted up, he will live."

Interviewer: Oh! So when he said that the Son of Man must be lifted up, he was talking about his crucifixion. He was saying that as he was lifted up on the cross, sinful people could see him and everyone who believes in his love for them will have everlasting life.

Nicodemus: Yes, and his resurrection must be told to all the world so that all peoples and nations can have eternal life. You know that God gave Jesus to the world because God loves the world so much that God wants everyone who believes in him not to perish but to have eternal life.

Interviewer: A lot of people today have a hard time accepting that God loves the whole world and everyone in it. Some people think that God picks and chooses who to love and who to condemn and that we should do the same.

Nicodemus: Don't forget what Jesus said next. He said, "God didn't send his Son into the world to judge the world, but that the world might be saved through him."

You see, we all are looking for something to save us from whatever stupid things we have done. We look for excuses. We try to shift blame. We claim ignorance. We project our faults onto others. We will do most anything not to be found guilty of our sins. As a Pharisee, I had spent my years trying to justify myself by keeping all the laws and condemning those who didn't. It didn't really matter who I might have hurt along the way. My attitude was, I don't really care about how hungry you are, I am going to say the proper prayer at the proper time. I am going to place the required offering on the altar on the correct day. I am not going to do anything but pray on the Sabbath, so don't try to get me to help you lift your donkey out of the well!

We all want to be saved from the punishment awaiting us when we die. But we are never sure if we have done enough to gain God's forgiveness. Jesus said he didn't come to judge the world or pass sentence on us. He came so that we might be saved.

"But how?" I thought.

"Just believe in me." Jesus said, "When I command you to love your neighbor and your enemy, do that. When I tell you to keep forgiving and stop counting how many times you have forgiven, just keep forgiving and trust that God will always forgive you. When I tell you to turn the other cheek or go an extra mile with someone who forces you to carry their burden one mile, do it and you will know that by giving more than is required of you, you will be stronger than if all you ever do is take."

Jesus left the city soon after that night.

Interviewer: Did you ever see him again?

Nicodemus: There was another time. Months later, Jesus returned to Jerusalem and by then his name had spread far and wide. A much larger crowd gathered around him when he taught in the temple courtyard. He was teaching them the same things he had talked about with me. He was warning them against judging each other. He was encouraging them to be more forgiving and more generous with the poor. He called out for everyone who was thirsty to come to him. He wasn't saying anything against the law.

The mob could not agree on what they wanted to do with him. Isn't that the way it always is with mobs? The Pharisees had sent guards to watch him and bring him in if necessary. When the guards returned without him the leaders shouted, "Where is he? Why isn't he with you?" All the captain of the guard said was, "We have never before heard anyone say the things he is saying."

Some of the leading Pharisees said, "Have you become believers as well? We don't believe in this guy – none of the Pharisees believe in him! The man is guilty of teaching against the law!"

I hesitated for a moment but I had to say something. I asked if any of them had ever spoken to Jesus. I told them that I had, and from what I heard, he was no threat to our precious law. I told them that he had talked to me about God's love for the whole world.

One of them jumped on that and argued, "Our God doesn't love the whole world. Our God is the God of the children of Abraham. This man is an enemy of our people and of God's law and he must be silenced."

"But our law doesn't judge someone without first hearing him and learning what he is doing, does it?" I said. They then asked if I was from Galilee. They said it sounded like I was supporting Jesus because he also was from Galilee. They said, "He cannot be the prophet from God if he is from Galilee." Rather than inviting Jesus to sit and discuss the law with them, they discussed plans for how they could trick Jesus into condemning himself in front of the people.

Interviewer: Was that the last time you saw Jesus?

Nicodemus: During the next l weeks, I saw Jesus several times. I never again spent time talking to him, but I heard a lot of what he told the people. He often spoke of his relationship with the Father. He said that God was in him and the things he said and did were the things the Father wanted him to teach them to do. He talked of forgiveness and love for each other.

Once they dragged a sinful woman before him. They were prepared to stone her. They told Jesus they had caught the woman in the act of adultery and that the Law of Moses dictated that she should be stoned. They wanted to know what Jesus would say should be done to her.

According to reports, Jesus said nothing. But he knelt down, placing himself between the woman and her accusers as he spoke softly to her. When they pressed him by reciting the law that said one who commits the sin of adultery must be stoned, Jesus stood up and faced them squarely and, looking into their eyes, said, "If any one of you has never sinned or broken one of the laws, let that one be the first to throw a stone." He then knelt down again next to the woman protecting her from whatever may come.

Not much was said after that. One by one, those leaders began to back off, drop their stones and drift away until there was no one left there but Jesus and the woman. It is reported by someone who remained close enough to hear that Jesus asked the woman, "Where are they? Is there anyone left condemning you?" She said, "No sir." Then Jesus said, "And I don't condemn you. Now go, and from now on, don't sin anymore."

You know the rest of the story of Jesus' arrest and execution. The last time I saw Jesus was when a wealthy friend of mine, a man named Joseph who was also a Pharisee, and I placed Jesus' dead body in a tomb Joseph owned near the place of the cross. I brought a large basket of burial spices to place on the body. When we were finished wrapping him with the spices, we rolled the large stone in front of the tomb until someone could return after the Sabbath to finish preparing him for final burial.

During that whole time I wondered what might have happened if I had been braver and had spoken up about believing in the things Jesus had been teaching. I wondered if my witness could have made a difference. I truly believed that the lessons Jesus shared were true. I knew that on those occasions when I went out of my way to help a stranger or when I let go of the anger I held against one who had wronged me, I felt much better about myself. And as I remembered the night Jesus told me that

God loved the whole world so much that he gave his only Son so that you and I could be forgiven for our sins and not judged by them or condemned for them, I felt a great peace wash over me.

In that dark moment as Joseph and I walked away from that grave, I somehow felt that would not be the end. God surely could not be finished with us. There must be more to come. And you know what happened next.

Interviewer: We certainly do! Thank you, Nicodemus for sharing your story.

Chapter 10

Pontius Pilate,
the governor
Luke 23:1-25

IN THE YEAR 26, JUDEA received its fifth Roman Governor – Pontius Pilate. As the name indicates, he was from the family "Pontii". The Pontiis were considered middle nobility during the period of the Roman Empire. The name "Pontius" means "skilled with the javelin." Pontius Pilate rose through the ranks of the military until he reached the rank of Equestrian. Little is known of him prior to his assignment to Judea. It is supposed that he had served a military command in the Germanic area around the Rhine or Danube. Pilate served ten years, from 26 to 36 CE as procurator, or governor in Judea, one of the longest tenures of any Roman governor.

Pilate brought his wife with him on his appointment to Judea. Her name, according to later Christian tradition, was Claudia Procula. No details are known of her, but it is supposed by some scholars that her advice to her husband to "wash his hands" of the whole affair concerning the accused Jesus indicates that she may have been a closet believer. We learn from Paul that many wives of Roman officials became believers.

One of the first acts of the new governor was to bring Roman banners into the temple at Jerusalem as a show of Roman power and presence. Since some of those banners, or standards, carried the image of the emperor, the Jews responded strongly against their presence in the temple. Jewish leaders sent a delegation to Caesarea where the governor resided. They waited several days for an audience with Pilate. What they got instead was a line of soldiers who surrounded them with swords drawn awaiting Pilate's order to attack. The Jewish leaders prostrated themselves on the ground and said they would rather die than allow their temple to be desecrated with pagan images. Pilate backed down and ordered the standards to be removed.

At another time, in an effort to address the inadequate water supply in Jerusalem, Pilate initiated a public works project of building an aqueduct to bring water into Jerusalem. He robbed the temple treasury to build the aqueduct. The Jewish leaders were furious! To quell the angry street demonstrations that broke out, Pilate had his soldiers dress in plain clothes and move about among the demonstrators. At a prearranged signal, the soldiers attacked using clubs. Many Jews were killed. The Jews never forgot this act of violent aggression. The Gospel of Luke tells us that Pilate murdered a group of Jews from Galilee while they were peacefully offering their sacrifices. (Luke 13:1-4)

The population of Jerusalem during Jesus' time

was estimated to be 600,000 by the Roman historian Tacitus. Each year during the Passover celebration, that number would swell to well over one million. Josephus estimates 2.5 million. Because of the constant threat of violent disturbances during that time, the governor would move from Caesarea to Jerusalem to maintain control. That is exactly what happened during the Passover that Jesus spent in Jerusalem during his final week.

Interviewer: Governor Pilate, what can you tell us about the atmosphere in Jerusalem in the year 30?

Pilate: As usual, for that time of the year, it was a tinder-box. When a city becomes that overcrowded with people from so many lands and cultures speaking so many languages, it doesn't take much of a spark to light things up! I didn't really care about who was right or who was wrong in any of their quarrels. My orders were to keep the peace and dispose of anyone who disturbed it.

I had soldiers stationed throughout the city on every rooftop, in every market, at every gate into the city and in the courtyard of their precious temple. I received regular reports from my centurions on the movements of the leading priests and lawyers. I had spies dressed in common threads moving about in the market places picking up on whatever gossip was circulating.

Interviewer: What sort of things were you hearing?

Pilate: The talk that year was mostly about a young firebrand of a preacher from the north who was gaining a lot of attention. There was talk of him becoming a new king of the Jews. That would mean trouble since Herod, the king appointed by Rome, would not go quietly if challenged.

Things were normally pretty quiet on Fridays and Saturdays since those were their days for worship and sacrifice. Sabbath, they called them. But on the day after the Sabbath, things were most likely to get lively when all their pent-up energy was let loose. And sure enough, on that Sunday, things got out of hand in a hurry.

I began to get reports that something was developing across the valley on the Olivet hill in the town of Bethany. I sent a squad of soldiers to make sure whatever was happening remained peaceful.

Interviewer: And did it?

Pilate: Thank the gods it did – at least for a while. The crowd paraded right up to the temple shouting and waving tree branches and cheering that young man. Though, I swear, as I caught a glimpse of him, he looked like anything but a wild rebel.

The next day, things apparently blew up in the temple market. He was back, but this time he went off on the stalls selling animals and on the licensed moneychangers. He had a whip of some sort and was on a rampage, turning over their stalls and chasing them out of the area. His friends were able to calm him down before the soldiers could get to him. Apparently, he was objecting to the slaughter of so many animals when he believed that all their God wanted was their prayers.

For the rest of the week, I doubled the guard in and around the temple and things appeared to stay calm. This Jesus, I learned, was going daily to the temple courtyard and teaching any who would listen, and a lot did! The Jewish leaders were becoming more and more concerned about the influence he was having on their people. They began plotting some way to silence him, but he was so popular that they were afraid to just arrest him and lose the support of the people.

As I now understand their plan, they identified one of his close followers who had expressed some dissatisfaction with Jesus, one named Judas. They bribed that fellow to find a time when Jesus would be away from the throngs of people and they could arrest him. On that Thursday night, after the Jews had all had their feasts, Judas came running to the temple and said he could lead the temple police to Jesus.

He led them across the Kidron Valley and up the Mt. of Olives to an old olive grove where Jesus was praying with his disciples. There were only ten or twelve of them, so the police had no trouble arresting him once Judas identified him with a typical kiss of greeting on his cheek. It was reported that Jesus just stood there for a minute looking at Judas, and then Jesus turned so Judas could kiss him on the other cheek as well.

My men reported that they first took Jesus to the High Priest's house where he was questioned most of the night. The next morning, they assembled their council of elders and questioned him further. After that is when they showed up at my door.

They were accusing Jesus of misleading the people – something about not following their laws, I guess. They also said he was telling the people not to pay the tax to the emperor. Their main point seemed to be that he was trying to pass himself off as a new king of the Jews.

So, I asked him, "Are you the king of the Jews?" All he could come up with was, "That's what you say." I turned to his accusers and told them I could find nothing wrong with the man. Then I heard one of them say something about Galilee and I inquired if he was from that region. I was tired of dealing with the matter, so when they said he was from up north, I hit on an idea. I knew that Antipas, who was in charge of that territory, was also in town for the holiday, so I ordered that they take him and their accusations to Herod.

In about an hour they were back saying that Herod wasn't willing to pass sentence on Jesus. I could tell though that Jesus had had a rough time at the hands of Herod's men. He was all bloodied and beat up and not standing quite as straight as before.

I gathered the Jewish leaders and told them that I found nothing about this man deserving death, which was apparently what they were seeking. I said, "And apparently neither did Herod since he sent him back here."

One of my advisors reminded me of the tradition that the governor release one prisoner to the Jews at Passover. I told the jailers to bring up the worst offender we had in custody. In a few minutes they returned with a brute named, coincidentally, Jesus Barabbas. Barabbas was an inciter of sedition and a murderer. He deserved to be locked up. I told them it was their choice – Jesus who was called "the Christ," or Jesus Barabbas. Their decision was immediate. They started calling out, "Barabbas! Release Barabbas!"

Then I asked them, "What should I do with Jesus, the Christ?"

"Kill him; crucify him!" they shouted."

"But why? What has he done?" I asked. They shouted even louder, "Crucify him!"

I could see the determination in their eyes and hear it in their shouts! They wanted Jesus crucified! I went back inside to where Jesus was being held and I asked him straight out, "Are you the king of the Jews?" He did not respond directly. He said, "Are you saying this because you believe it, or are others telling you this about me?

I said, "I'm not a Jew. Your own nation and its chief priests brought you to me. Tell me what have you done?"

Jesus then said, "My kingdom doesn't originate from this world. If it did, my angels would fight so that I wouldn't have been arrested by the Jewish leaders. My kingdom isn't from here."

"So you are a king?" I said. Jesus answered, "You say that I am a king. I was born and came into this world for a reason."

"And what might that reason be?" I asked.

"To testify to the truth," he said calmly. "Whoever accepts the truth listens to my voice."

"Ahh, but what is the truth?" I asked in exasperation. "Is power truth? Is wealth truth? Is wisdom truth?" He gave me no answer.

About that time, I was handed a note my wife Claudia sent me telling me to leave Jesus alone and have nothing to do with his death. She said she had been having powerful dreams about him all that day. I may have been the governor, but I have learned that my wife is very perceptive, and if she thought this was a bad thing, I was not going to risk disagreeing with her. I had my suspicions that the chief priests were the ones behind whipping up the crowd to call for Barabbas and to kill the Galilean.

Wanting to demonstrate some solidarity with the people, I sent Jesus out to be flogged by the soldiers, hoping that would satisfy them. When they brought him back, I could see that they had had some fun with him. He had been viciously whipped and had a circle of thorns pressed down on his head as though it were a crown. They had even draped some old piece of purple cloth over his shoulders like it was a king's robe. I took him out on the balcony and sarcastically said, "Here is your king!"

Interviewer: Why didn't you just stop the whole thing?

Pilate: I suppose I could tell you it was because I didn't really care, but I did. I knew Jesus was innocent and should be released, but I couldn't risk having the crowd turn against me. My career and my future was on the line. The fact is, I wasn't sure I knew what I was feeling. The crowd was chanting, "Crucify him," over and over. I knew they could have easily become violent and out of control and that would have ended in bloodshed and charges brought against me to the emperor. I could lose my post and be sent to Gaul or some other miserable outpost. I didn't want that.

But there was something about that man that I couldn't put my finger on. I decided to take Claudia's advice and wash my hands of the whole affair. I declared to the crowd, "I am innocent of this man's blood. He's now your problem." Then I released Barabbas and had Jesus whipped again and turned over to be crucified.

Interviewer: What were you feeling at that point?

Pilate: I shouldn't have been feeling anything. I had just done my job. I had kept the peace. I was just following orders. But there was something about that man that was different. I mean, there he was facing execution for "crimes" he hadn't done. Any other man would be pleading his own innocence and telling me his side of the story. Any other man would have been on his knees begging me for compassion and mercy.

But Jesus just stood there looking at me. It was as if he were trying to get me to look at myself and find my true strength – not the strength to destroy but the strength and courage to do what I knew was right. His eyes mesmerized me. I knew that by doing nothing I had done a great wrong.

All that happened on Friday. About three or four o'clock they came and told me that he was dead. I asked them if he ever said anything. They said that he promised one of the two thieves who were being crucified at the same time that he would be in heaven with him. They also said that at one point, he called out for his God to forgive all of them – all the ones who were crucifying him.

The centurion who was on duty said, with some trepidation, "Sir, I think that man might have been the Son of God as his people were claiming."

The next day was the day of worship for the Jews, so I never expected to receive a delegation of their leaders. But they came to me early and told me that while he was alive, Jesus had talked about rising from the dead in three days. They wanted me to order the grave where his followers had placed him to be sealed and guarded. They were afraid that his friends might come and steal the body and then spread the rumor that he was alive and that would make the situation worse than it already was.

I was not about to get sucked back into this situation. I told them that they had their own temple soldiers and guards. "Send them and do whatever you think is necessary." Later, I was told that they did just that. They sealed the tomb with a mix of Roman cement and posted a guard day and night at the entrance. Then, the Passover having ended, I returned to Caesarea and tried to forget that man's face looking at me with pity for my soul and not fear for his own.

Interviewer: Was that the last contact you had with Jesus?

Pilate: I wish that were so. I never saw him again face-to-face, but I never stopped seeing him in my dreams and in my thoughts, day and night. It wasn't but a few days later when my spies told me that people were claiming he was alive and being seen by large crowds all around the territory. Now and then, Claudia would tell me about something she had heard he was doing.

I could never get past the guilt I felt for not doing anything to spare him, especially since I knew at the time that would have been the right thing to do. I could have said or done something to make a difference. I just didn't. I kept hearing him pray for forgiveness for those who were crucifying him and I wondered if that could somehow include me!

I didn't know much about the God they worshipped, but I heard Claudia talk often about their God being a forgiving God and that we need to forgive others if we want peace.

"Peace?" I would shout back to her, "Rome is all about peace. My job is to keep the peace. The Peace of Rome is official government policy. Everyone just keep quiet and pay your taxes and there will be peace. Peace at the tip of the sword!"

"But," she would say, "that is peace based on fear, and your job is to keep fear in the hearts of these people. They aren't living in peace, they are living in fear – of you." I knew she was correct. But I was just following orders. What else could I do?

Interviewer: Your tenure as Perfect, or Governor of Judea lasted ten years – longer than most other such appointments. Just two years after Jesus' crucifixion, there is another report of your vicious treatment of a mob. This time it happened in Samaria.

Pilate: That's right. A deranged Samaritan "prophet" gathered a mob on Mt. Gerizim where he said Moses had buried a great treasure. I sent my auxiliaries to put a stop to what easily could have become an open revolt. The soldiers formed a line to stop the advance of an armed force of several hundred Samaritans. When the Samaritans tried to break through the line, Roman soldiers responded with all the weapons at their disposal. Hundreds of the Samaritans were slaughtered.

I was recalled to stand before Emperor Tiberius as a result of that massacre. A delegation of Samaritans and Jews had travelled to Rome to complain about what they said was my excessively violent treatment of the people. However, Tiberius died while I was in route to Rome.

Interviewer: There is no evidence that Pilate ever got his hearing before an emperor. In fact, there is no definitive account of what happened to Pilate after that. Some traditions say he was demoted and reassigned to an unimportant outpost in the frigid north countries. A perhaps more reliable tradition holds that he took his own life as a result of the unrelenting guilt he carried for what he had done and failed to do in his encounter with Jesus.

In one way Pontius Pilate and Jesus were not that different. They both were after the same goal – peace. Peace is a natural desire of humans. As a soldier and political leader, Pilate was committed to the policy known as the Pax Romana, the Peace of Rome. The Roman Empire grew through the use of violent military action against tribes living in the areas Rome wished to annex. Those encounters were terribly if not excessively violent. But that level of excessive violence was an intentional plan meant to leave a permanent reminder in the minds of the conquered tribes of what Rome could do, and as an incentive to keep quiet and complacent. That was Roman peace.

Jesus, as well, was a promoter of peace. In Jesus mind, peace was not fearful compliance to an enemy who is holding a sword to your neck.

To Jesus' way of thinking, peace comes when all fear is gone. Peace results from the elimination of all that frightens, intimidates, or threatens us. Peace is not feeling isolated or alone, which is why Jesus' promise to be with us always is so vital and is repeated over and over in the gospels.

Peace is possible only when we know we are loved. Peace is possible when we feel that our lives are valued. Peace comes when we know that we do not need to live in fear of punishment for the evil and damaging things we have done, because we are forgiven by the One who chooses to love rather than to punish.

Peace comes when the fear of death is removed. The one fear that all of us share at some level or another is the fear of death. What happens when we die? Anything? Jesus told us to not be afraid or troubled by thoughts of dying. Jesus promised that life continues after the death of our bodies. Jesus tells us that the Father has places prepared for us in his heavenly dwelling. That is the peace of Christ.

We don't know if Pilate ever heard that message from Jesus. We do know that God gave him a wife who likely heard it, and we can only hope she had the courage to share it with her husband.

Chapter 11

Mary Magdalene,
first to the tomb
Luke 8:1-3

In his second book, The Acts of the Apostles, Dr. Luke gives his account of the disciples replacing the betrayer, Judas, with a "thirteenth" disciple. The one qualification that they stipulated for those being considered was that they had "accompanied Jesus during the whole time the Lord Jesus lived among them beginning from his baptism by John until the day when Jesus was taken from them." Matthias was elected to the position. However, we learn from their stated qualification that there must have been others who had traveled with Jesus from the beginning of his ministry in Galilee through to the crucifixion and resurrection. Our interview this day will be with one of those other disciples who knew Jesus from the start. Her name is Mary.

Since there are no fewer than six woman with the name of Mary in the New Testament, including Jesus' own mother, you will need a little more information about today's guest in order to correctly identify her.

The Mary we will be interviewing today comes from a small town on the northwest shore of the Galilean lake. Her town sits between Tiberius and Capernaum. The town of Magdala was a fish processing center for the fishing industry on the lake. There was a "fish-tower" there for drying and salting fish and preparing it for sale to homes and markets.

To the south of Magdala was the relatively new city of Tiberias, founded by Herod Antipas. Tiberias was the capital of Galilee between 17 and 20 CE. Like all new capital cities, we can only imagine there was a high level of energy in Tiberias. There must have been constant construction going on. There were important and international travelers coming and going. There was wealth and there were tourists. Just to the south of Tiberias, also on the shore of the lake, there was (and still is) a natural therapeutic hot spring that attracts travelers from far and near.

North of Magdala, also on the shore of the lake, is the city of Capernaum. Capernaum was a fishing village and was the home of Peter and Andrew and James and John, and the home of Jesus and his family after they left Nazareth.

People from Magdala were known as "Magdalenes," as was our guest for today's interview – Mary Magdalene.

Interviewer: Good morning Mary. We are so glad to have you with us today. Did I get all that information correct?

Mary: It is my pleasure to be with you, and, yes, that was all accurate.

Interviewer: I'm glad. Since you were with Jesus longer than most of the other early believers, you must have more stories than the others. We would like for you to tell us about some of your experiences travelling with Jesus, and especially about the events leading up to the day we call Easter.

First, though, how did you get to know Jesus?

Mary: My father was in the fish processing business. Every day he would make the trip around the shore of the lake buying fish from the boats when they would return to the docks. As I got older, he would take me with him to help load the barrels of fish onto his wagon. We would stop at Gennesarat then Ginnesar, Capernaum, and the last stop was Bethsaida at the very north tip of the lake where the waters of the Jordan flow in from Lake Huleh and Mt. Hermon way up north.

One day when we reached the docks at Capernaum, all the fishing boat crews were gathered around one young man who was telling stories. My father and I listened for a while and we were enthralled! I remember the man saying that the kingdom of heaven was like a net thrown into the sea and gathered in full of fish of every kind. Sensing that he was really talking about people and not fish, I really liked the picture he painted with his words. I liked thinking about a place where all kinds of people could live together and not fight with each other.

He often spoke about God's kingdom or the kingdom of Heaven. For a long time I didn't know what he was talking about. But I knew that neither the Jews nor the Romans would tolerate any talk of a king or kingdom that wasn't their own. The thing they all seemed to fear most was any threat to their power. The Romans would often make crowds of Jews shout, "We have no king but King Caesar!" I knew that Jesus was saying dangerous things when he talked about the kingdom of God.

At that time I was about fifteen years old and I was what you might call a "wild child!" It seems I was always causing some mischief or getting into some kind of trouble; often it was with boys.

At one point it got so bad that my father would no longer take me with him to buy the fish. He said that it was embarrassing to hear the gossip people were spreading about his daughter. He was afraid it would hurt his business if they didn't stop. The only thing he could do to stop them was to just not have me around while he was conducting business. I was so hurt, but I knew he was right. I tried to behave, but I kept doing bad things.

I had heard that Jesus could change people and I knew that I needed to be changed! I also heard that he could forgive people their sins. I so wanted to get close to him and ask for his forgiveness, but there didn't seem to be a way.

Then one day the word on the street was that Jesus was going to be having dinner with one of the Pharisees in our town. I made a plan to be at that dinner. I dressed like one of the servants. I poured some of mother's scented oil into a small alabaster jar and tucked it into my girdle. When everyone was seated at the table with their feet behind them as was custom, I came up behind Jesus without anyone noticing. I was so scared that I began to cry. I let my tears fall onto his feet and began gently rubbing his feet with my hair. Then I poured the oil on his feet and kissed them.

By that time, others had noticed what I was doing. The Pharisee host said to Jesus, "If you knew what kind of girl this is, you wouldn't let her touch you. She is a sinner."

Jesus replied, "Simon, a certain leader had two debtors who owed him money. One owed enough to pay five hundred people for a day's work. The other owed enough for fifty days wages. When it came time to pay off their debts, neither man could pay. The man to whom the money was owed forgave the debt of both. Which one of them will love the man more?"

Simon thought for a moment and then said, "I suppose the one who had the largest debt cancelled." Jesus told him that he was right. Then Jesus turned to me and said to Simon, "Do you see this woman? When I entered your home, you didn't give me water for my feet, but she wet my feet with her tears and wiped them with her hair. You didn't greet me with a kiss, but she hasn't stopped kissing my feet since I came in. You didn't anoint my head with oil, but she has poured very expensive perfumed oil on my feet. I tell you that her many sins have been forgiven because she has shown great love. Then he turned to me and said, "Mary, your sins are forgiven and your faith has saved you. Go in peace."

I asked Jesus how God could forgive the terrible things I had done. Jesus said that God forgives every sin. That there is no sin so great that God hasn't already forgiven it. He said, "All you have to do is receive God's love and love others the way I am loving you."

After that I changed. Or I should say, I was changed. I knew that Jesus thought I could be better than I had been and his confidence made me believe the same thing. I began to hang out with Jesus' growing group of disciples and some others who had also been forgiven by Jesus. One day, as he began to talk about going around to the villages of Galilee and then on to Jerusalem, he pulled me aside and invited me to accompany them. I was never so thrilled and honored. I was a nobody, just a sinful girl. I immediately said, "Yes!"

It turned out that there were other women in the group including Joanna, the wife of one of Herod's servants, and Susanna, from Capernaum. As we travelled, the four of us women and others gladly took on the responsibility of preparing meals for the whole group. Those of us who could used our own money to buy the food and supplies.

One of the things I remember most about those days is the stories Jesus told. He had the ability to teach a lesson with just a few words, like the time he told of a farmer scattering seed. As we all knew, some of the seed would fall on the hard-worn path where the farmer was standing, some in the thistles and some on the good soil. But then Jesus likened the path to people whose hearts were so hard they could not accept a new thing if it was given to them. The thorny plants were the people who never did anything but disagree and argue and choke the life out of any new idea. Of course, the good soils were the people whose hearts and minds are open to receive the seed that will grow to new life in them. I think he was telling us to look at ourselves and see if we were open to his new teaching or not.

Everywhere we went, there were sick people and he took time to heal as many of them as he could; but he was always reminding them and us that more important than the healing of bodies was the message of God's love that heals the heart. He not only talked about how we should love neighbors and enemies, he showed us every day as he spoke to all the different kinds of people we met. He would stop and talk to Roman soldiers at the city gates. He would spend time with the tax collectors who had sold out our people to work for Rome. And the children! He loved the children.

I can still see him stopping to join a game of kick-ball out in a field with a bunch of kids. It gave him such pleasure and it made the kids feel special to have someone so important play with them. He would always stop and call the little ones who were hiding behind their momma's skirts to come over and tell him their names and laugh and joke with them.

One time he picked up a child, with the child's mother's permission of course, and came and sat down with that child in the middle of the circle of his disciples. Knowing that there had been discussions among the twelve about who he liked the best and who would be the greatest in God's kingdom, he looked around and said that that child would be the greatest in the kingdom of heaven and all those who became like children would be the greatest because God likes the way children are so open and loving and giving and forgiving.

He was never too busy for the sick and the hurting and the children.

Interviewer: Mary, before we run out of time, can you tell us about the time in Jerusalem?

Mary: Yes, thank you for reminding me. There is so much more that happened, but let's move on to that last week in Jerusalem.

By the time we passed through Jericho and began the ascent up to Jerusalem, our numbers had swollen into the hundreds with folks who had heard Jesus and had become believers. From time to time, Jesus had talked about being arrested and killed in Jerusalem. We thought he was talking in metaphors like when he talked about the farmer and the seeds. Little did we know at the time just how real his words would prove to be.

The day following the Sabbath prior to the Passover, we were in the village of Bethany on the Mount of Olives, overlooking the Temple and the city. Jesus sent two of his disciples into the city to obtain a small donkey for him to ride. While we waited, I saw Jesus tear up and mumble a prayer for the city asking God to forgive its people for not knowing the things that make for peace and for not recognizing the presence of God in their midst. He was visibly moved.

When they returned with the animal and we began to descend into the valley, the crowd began to get really excited. A celebration broke out with singing and shouting. Palm branches were being waved overhead and crowds lined up all along the road into Jerusalem. It was an exciting moment.

The week was filled with preparations for the Passover feast. Daily, Jesus and a small group of friends went to the temple where he would spend hours teaching and healing those who came to him. On Thursday, we gathered upstairs in the home of a lovely, believing family. The meal was prepared and served. The Passover story was read and the dinner was eaten. That's when things began to take an unexpected turn.

When it was time for the bread, Jesus broke the loaf in two and said, "This bread has always been eaten without yeast to remind us of the day when God delivered his people out of slavery in Egypt. But from now on, I want my people to let the broken bread remind you of the sacrifice of my body, broken for you for your deliverance from sin and death." As the bread was being passed around, Jesus startled us by saying, "One of you will betray me." There was an audible gasp that went up from all of us at the table. Then the questions, "Who is it Lord?" "Is it I?" During the commotion and chatter, I noticed Judas slip out of the room, and I wondered.

After the supper, when Jesus held up the cup, he said, "And I want this wine to remind you of my blood which soon will be poured out for you and for all people for the forgiveness of your sins." The way he said it, it didn't sound metaphorical.

After we sang a hymn, Jesus asked to be excused and took the eleven disciples with him. They were going out to pray, Jesus said. The family that was hosting us had a teenaged son who was apparently sent by his father to follow Jesus and report back if there was any trouble.

After we cleaned up and put the dishes and food away, we sat down to visit with our hosts. We learned that the wife's name was also Mary. It wasn't too long before the boy, named John Mark, came running in and shouting that Jesus had been arrested! Soon the others came back to the house telling how Judas, the one who left the table, had led a contingent of temple guards to the garden where Jesus was and how he identified him to the soldiers with a kiss. Mark said there was a scuffle and one of the guards caught hold of his clothes, but he was able to slip out of what he was wearing and run away.

Soon the others also returned, but no one knew what had happened to Jesus after that. Peter told the rest of us to stay locked in the upstairs room while he went to find Jesus. Those were frightening hours while we waited. To try to calm things down, I suggested that we each share the favorite story we had heard from Jesus.

I told the story of the wealthy woman who lost one coin. Her friends told her not to worry about it, she had plenty more. But the woman could not do that and she swept her whole house over and over until she found the one lost coin. When she found it, she threw a party and invited all her friends to celebrate with her. I chose that story because when Jesus told it, I felt like he was talking about me. I too was wealthy, but there was a part of my life that felt so lost. And then I found Jesus, and the way he forgave me and included me in his circle of friends as though I was important made me a different and much richer person. He told me that God is also like that woman. God has all things, but God wants even me and will not stop searching until he has brought me home.

Just after sunup, Peter came back telling us that the soldiers were on their way to Pilate to have him issue the order for Jesus' execution. He also said that there were orders issued to arrest any of the other men who were with Jesus. I said, "I'm going. If he sees me, perhaps that will bring him some comfort." Some of the other women said the same thing and we headed out in the direction of the Fortress of Antonia where Pilate lodged while in the city. That fortress was adjacent to the temple.

By the time we got there, we could hear the sounds of the soldiers flogging a prisoner. When they next brought him out to stand before Pilate, we saw it was Jesus. He looked so pitiful. The governor said that he could find no fault in Jesus, certainly not anything that would call for his execution. He offered to release him as a show of good faith to the city. But the crowd, as if on cue, began to shout, "Crucify him! We have no king but Caesar!"

Pilate, the coward that he was, said, "Okay. Do what you want with him. I want nothing to do with this man." Then, as if it would make a difference, Pilate plunged his hands into a bowl of water and cried out, "I wash my hands of him! I am innocent of his blood!"

They made Jesus carry the crossbeam through the streets to the place where they routinely executed prisoners.

When he got to the point where we were in the throng, he stopped and turned to us and said, "Daughters of Jerusalem, don't cry for me. Rather, cry for yourselves and your children. The days are coming when those who were never able to bear children will be the fortunate ones."

While they were nailing him to the cross and hoisting it in place, they made the crowd of mourners and onlookers stand back so we couldn't see the violence involved in that process. But when the cross was raised and secure in the hole in the ground, they let any who wanted to come close. Close enough so the condemned could hear their jeers and cursing. Close enough so the crowd could throw rocks at the prisoners. It was a gruesome sight.

We were finally able to get through the crowds to the foot of Jesus' cross. He was in such pain! When he saw his mother, he pleaded for John to take care of her as though she were his own mother. Jesus spoke several times from the cross, but the thing I remember most that he said was when he lifted his face to the heavens and cried out, "Father, forgive these people. They have no idea what they are doing." For anyone who knew him, those were not surprising words. He knew we were all sinners of one degree or another and that we all stood in need of forgiveness. But to include the men who had whipped him, who had pressed the crown of thorns down on his head, even the man standing there holding the hammer that had driven the nails – that was typical of Jesus. He loved even his enemies!

After about three hours it was over. We watched as the life slowly drained from him. A soldier came along and thrust a spear into his side to see if he was still pumping blood. He was not.

A couple of Pharisees came along with some helpers to take him down. They assured us they were friends and would see to it that he got a proper burial. We followed them to the tomb where they wrapped him and laid him out on the slab that was there. Then they rolled a great stone to seal the opening. We returned to the house and told the others all that had happened.

That Sabbath was a sad and silent one. No one wanted to speak. No one could believe what had happened. No one knew what to do next.

Interviewer: What did you do?

Mary: We cried. We prayed all day and night. I stayed still as long as I could, and then sometime before daylight, I got up and began to gather what I could find to prepare his body. It wasn't long before his mother was also up. Joanna heard us moving around and got up as well. We didn't have much to work with as we had not come prepared for a burial.

But it turned out that his mother had brought with her a beautiful pouch that we never knew she had. She told us that she had had it since Jesus was born and had kept it for this very moment. She said it was a gift from some visitors who came to the cave where she gave birth. She said it was frankincense and myrrh to anoint his body.

Without giving much thought as to what we would do when we got there, we made our way through the silent streets of Jerusalem to the tomb on the other side of the city.

Now, I know you know what happened next. But just put yourselves in our place. It was dark. We were frightened. There was a small earthquake. We were trying to see through the light rain and the early morning mist. We saw the tomb and supposed we saw the stone covering the opening. But as we got closer, there was no stone. The tomb had been opened! There was a squad of soldiers, but they were all sleeping.

Then it appeared as though there were two men, all dressed in white, standing at the door of the tomb. They said, as with one voice, "Why are you looking for the living among the dead? He isn't here, he has been raised!" They reminded us that he had said that the Son of Man must be crucified but that he would rise on the third day.

We turned and ran back to the house where we reported all that we had seen and heard to the others. We could tell they didn't believe us. But Peter and John grabbed their cloaks and ran out. I followed as closely as I could, but they got there before I did. They both stepped inside the tomb and saw that it was empty. All they saw were the cloths that Jesus body had been wrapped in.

I was standing outside crying when they came out of the tomb and left. In a moment I bent down to look into the tomb. I saw the two men in white that I had seen the first time. They asked me, "Why are you crying?" I said, "They have taken away my Lord, and I don't know where they have put him." As soon as I said that, I heard a quiet rustling behind me. I turned around and saw a man standing there, but I didn't recognize him at first. I thought he might be the gardener. Then he said to me, "Woman, why are you crying? Who are you looking for?"

I said, "I am looking for my Lord. If you have carried him away, tell me where you have put him and I will get him." That's when the man I was looking at said quietly, "Mary." It was him! It was Jesus! He was alive and talking to me! I said, "Teacher!" as I reached out to hold him. But he said, "Don't hold on to me, for I haven't yet gone up to my Father. But go to my brothers and sisters and tell them I am going up to my Father and your Father, to my God and your God."

I didn't want to leave that place or that moment, but Jesus had given me instructions for what I should do, and I did it. I went to the others and shouted, "I have seen the Lord!" I told them what he had said about going up to the Father. Others went to the tomb and returned to verify that it was open and empty.

That evening we were all gathered in the upper room when suddenly Jesus was standing there with us. "Peace be with you," is what he said. Then he showed us the wounds in his hands and side. At that, we all believed. Then Jesus said, "Peace be with you. As the Father has sent me, so I am sending you." Then he breathed on us and said, "Receive the Holy Spirit. If you forgive anyone's sins they are forgiven; if you don't forgive them, they aren't forgiven." And then he was gone.

Interviewer: But you did see him again, didn't you?

Mary: We did see him again. The following week we were all gathered again in the upper room, only this time, Thomas, who had been absent the week prior, was with us. We were describing to him what had happened, but he was not really believing us. But then Jesus was suddenly in the room again. He was patient with Thomas and let him touch his wounds and encouraged him to believe. Thomas shouted, "My Lord and my God. I do believe!"

For the next month, Jesus was with us and showed himself to hundreds of people before we watched as he was taken up into heaven. Everybody who saw him told others. Once again, Jesus made me feel so special by appearing to me first after he rose from the grave! I hope you have seen him as well. If not, invite him into your heart and you will see him.

Interviewer: Thank you Mary. You have made us feel special by sharing your story with us.

Chapter 12

James, brother of Jesus
Acts 15:13-21; 21:18

IN THIS CHAPTER WE WILL be privileged to interview James, the brother of Jesus. Before we get started, I want to mention one significant point in determining the dynamics of the family of James and Jesus. According to the Gospel accounts, Jesus was the first child of Mary. Matthew and Mark both tell us that Jesus had brothers and sisters and that one of the brothers was named James. (Matthew 13:55; Mark 6:3) In both of these lists, James is the first son listed, perhaps an indication of birth order? If that is accurate then we generally assume that Mary and Joseph had several other children (boys and girls) after Jesus, making Jesus the oldest son.

However, in support of the Catholic doctrine of the "perpetual virginity of Mary," the church in later centuries proposed the idea that when Joseph took Mary for his wife he was already an old man with grown children from a previous marriage. If true, this would mean that Jesus was the youngest child, and several years younger than Joseph's eldest son, James. That would change the family dynamic from Jesus' perspective – from being the oldest child to the youngest of several siblings.

With no other verifying evidence, we are going to proceed based on the account found in the Gospels. Jesus was the first born of Mary. Mary and Joseph and Jesus spent two or three years in Egypt after Jesus' birth and when they returned, there is no mention of other children with them. Jesus was, therefore, likely three or four years older than James (maybe more) with the others trailing behind.

Interviewer: Brother James we are honored to have you with us today.

James: It is my privilege. I imagine that you want to hear about the struggles we went through in the first years of the developing church.

Interviewer: Yes, we know you were in leadership during that time. But first, could you tell us about growing up in Nazareth with the family?

James: Oh, those were good times. It was hectic, at times chaotic, but it was good. Eventually there were seven of us kids and with mother and father there were nine of us living in one small house. There was only one room with blankets hung to create private spaces for our parents and for the girls. At night the animals came inside and found a place to sleep – chickens and goats mostly.

When Jesus was old enough, father would take him to

work with him as a sort of informal apprentice. I was put in charge of the other children during the day. Mother was the teacher and I was the organizer of activities to keep the little ones busy and out of trouble. In the evenings, Jesus would often tell stories to the younger ones. We loved the way he would tell about everyday normal things such as bread or trees or sheep, but always give them wonderful meanings. There was always a message about the love of God in his stories, a message that would be a lesson for all of us, not just the little ones.

Sometime after our father died, Jesus told mother and me that he needed to go away and share what he knew about God's love with other people. Mother was worried about him traveling alone, but he assured her that he would take some friends with him. Then he turned to me and told me that I was old enough and skilled enough to take over the business and support the family. I had my fears of such responsibility, but his confidence gave me the courage to believe him when he said that I could do it.

Interviewer: How often did you see your brother after that?

James: Oh, we saw him often. Jesus and his group of friends would come back to Capernaum often after visiting some of the smaller towns in Galilee. Finally, on one of those visits, he told me that he was going to be heading down to Jerusalem and very possibly not coming back. He said he planned to be there for the Passover and asked me to bring mother so we could all be together. I agreed and then I didn't see him again until we gathered for the Passover feast in the home of some of his friends.

I know you know well the story of that amazing weekend when Jesus was crucified and rose up from the dead, so I will skip to the events following the time of his ascent into the Father's glory.

There were something over a hundred disciples, followers, and family members who had heard and believed in Jesus' teachings about how God loves us and how we ought to love others – including the Romans! We remained in the upper room in the home of John Mark's family, partly out of fear of the Romans, but mostly because, in his last words, Jesus directed us to remain in Jerusalem and wait for the Father's Holy Spirit to come to us.

Each day we would gather what we could from the food we had and some would go out to the streets and give it away to the poor. Our numbers grew daily as people responded to the love they were being shown.

After Peter's fiery message on that Pentecost day, thousands wanted to be a part of the "Jesus Movement" as we were being called. We soon had to put a little organization to the "movement." We selected seven young men to serve the food and make sure it was distributed fairly with no preference shown to one group or another. Peter and John and his brother James were the natural leaders because Jesus had confided in them more than the others. They wanted me to be part of the leadership council since I was Jesus' brother.

It wasn't long before our growing numbers and

influence among the people drew the suspicion of the authorities. They arrested and killed young Stephen, one of the seven chosen to serve the meals. They employed agents to go around and gather up our people to harass us. They got hold of James, the brother of John, and Herod had him killed with a sword. When he saw that this pleased the Jews, he arrested Peter as well. But, with the help of an angel, as Peter told it, he was able to escape from the jail.

The followers of Jesus began to remove themselves to other towns just to get away from the troubles. But the troubles followed them, especially in the person of one Saul. Saul was the fiercest opponent of the message of Jesus and the most determined to silence us.

But the movement grew and became stronger. You know of the amazing thing that happened to Saul. How he had a vision of the risen Lord and became a dynamic preacher of the message. At first there was significant doubt about his claim to be a believer. Paul, as he was called after that, was sent home to his city in Cilicia where he spent several years before Barnabas sent for him. Barnabas was planning to travel to Cyprus, his home, to tell the story of Jesus. Barnabas also took his young cousin John Mark in whose home we had been meeting since the last supper we had with Jesus.

During that time, Peter and I became the recognized leaders of the movement that came to be called "the church." At one time, Peter felt led by a vision he had where the voice of God told him to eat an unclean and prohibited animal. Peter said that when he objected to violating the law, he heard the voice telling him that when the Father calls something good and worthy, we have no right to call it otherwise. Peter then said that he was led to the home of a Roman Centurion who was desiring baptism in the name of Jesus for himself and his family. Peter told them the good news of Jesus' promise of life after death for those who love God and love each other. Before he left, he said that Cornelius, the centurion, asked that he baptize the entire household, which he did.

When we heard about what Peter had done, not everyone was happy with his decision to bring Gentiles into the fellowship of the church. They said that, because Jesus was Jewish, everyone should become Jewish before becoming a follower. I believe that way of thinking and the division that event caused in the church plagues the people of Jesus even into your day.

Interviewer: Sadly, you are right. The churches today are still fussing and fighting over whom we think God wants us to let into the church and whom we should keep out.

James: The issue came to a head when Paul returned from one of his extended journeys through the Gentile lands of the Greeks. He told about all the different peoples he had preached to and how many of them had become baptized believers and accepted Jesus as their Lord and Savior. He told about women who had preached and led clusters of new followers. He told about a young doctor who had listened to him and subsequently became a wonderful help in the ministry. But even with his glowing and triumphant reports, there were many who believed that because the Messiah God sent had been a circumcised Jew, all who came after him must also first become circumcised Jews before they could be welcomed into the fellowship of Jesus' community.

At the very first conference of Church leaders from across Palestine, that was the primary topic of discussion. Peter was there and told about his experience with Cornelius and his family. Paul and Barnabas were there and told amazing stories of the acceptance of Jesus' name among the non-Jewish Greeks and Romans and others. Finally, after much arguing, it was agreed that we should not put a stumbling block such as circumcision before any who wanted to come into the church. As leader of that church council, I wrote a letter for Paul to take with him in case some of those who opposed our decision tried to interfere with his mission. Let me read that letter to you:

> The apostles and the elders, to the Gentile brothers and sisters in Antioch, Syria, and Cilicia. Greetings!
>
> We've heard that some of our number have disturbed you with unsettling words we didn't authorize. We reached a united decision to select some delegates and send them to you along with our dear friends Barnabas and Paul.
>
> These people have devoted their lives to the name of our Lord Jesus Christ. Therefore, we are sending Judas and Silas. They will confirm what we have written. The Holy Spirit has led us to the

decision that no burden should be placed on you
other than these essentials: refuse food offered to
idols, blood, the meat from strangled animals,
and sexual immorality. You will do well to avoid
such things. Farewell.

(Acts 15:23-29)

When Peter reported on his visit to the home of the
Roman Centurion, he concluded by saying, "I really am
learning that God doesn't show partiality to one group
of people over another. Rather, in every nation, whoever
worships him and does what is right is acceptable to him."

When Peter addressed that first conference, he said,
"Early on, God chose me from among you as the one
through whom the Gentiles would hear the word of the
gospel and come to believe. God gave them the Holy Spirit,
just as he did to us. He made no distinction between us
and them, but purified their deepest thoughts and desires
through faith. Why then are you now challenging God
by placing a burden on the shoulders of these disciples . . .
we believe that we and they are saved in the same way, by
the grace of the Lord Jesus."

As Peter was speaking, I remember thinking, "If Jesus
invites people of all nations and all walks of life into his
family, who are we to deny full fellowship with some of
those we don't like?"

Shortly after that, Paul headed out again on another
of his journeys. Others went journeying as well. Philip
went into Samaria and ended up settling in Capernaum

where he raised four wonderful daughters who were very active in the ministry of the church.

Andrew travelled north into what you know as Turkey, Kazakhstan, Turkmenistan, Iran, Russia and likely, even Poland.

Matthew is believed by some to have traveled to Russia after having written his Gospel in Antioch. In fact, there is a series of caverns in Kyrgyzstan that locals identify as the final resting place of the bones of the Gospel writer.

We are fairly certain that Thomas ended up in India where he had a very productive ministry. In your day there are still Christians in India who call themselves "Thomas Christians" and worship in sanctuaries they believe he built.

John took our mother, Mary, with him to Ephesus on the eastern shore of the Aegean Sea. There, John built a church whose remains can still be visited. Tradition has it that John and possibly Mary both died in that place. However, there are at least three other sites that claim to be the final resting place of Mary.

Interviewer: And what about you. Did you also travel to distant places?

James: As for me, I remained in Jerusalem. Once Peter was taken away to Rome, I was seen as the leading pastor of the faith since I was the brother of the Lord. We continued the best way we could to gather enough food to keep the hungry fed, to comfort the sick. We prayed over the sick and made sure the widows and orphans were cared for. We prayed daily and observed the Sabbath, though, from the beginning, it was our practice to pray through the night on the last day of the week until sunrise on the first day of the week, the day of resurrection.

When Paul returned from his third extensive journey deep into the heart of the Gentile lands, he gave us a detailed report of what God had done among the Gentiles through his ministry. He told of visiting the Jewish synagogues when he arrived in a town, and if there was no synagogue, he asked around until he identified the local place of prayer of the Jews. His approach was that they were Jews, he was a Jew, and all Jews were awaiting the Messiah that God would send. Then he told them that the Messiah had come in the person of Jesus in the land of Israel. He told them about the promise that Jesus had made for everlasting life for all people who would follow his singular rule to love: love God and love neighbor.

He reported some successes, but also some problems. His biggest opposition, he said, came from those who believed that you cannot be a follower of Jesus unless you first become Jewish. He said that he told the people that in Jesus there is no Jew or Greek, no slave or freedman, no wealthy or poor, no male or female. He preached that Jesus loves all people and wants all people to be together in his family. Some of the Jewish leaders, he said, just could not accept that. When he could not get a hearing among the Jews, he turned to the gentiles where he was enthusiastically welcomed.

By the way, you will be interested to know that the young doctor named Luke who had been travelling with

Paul came to Jerusalem with him and I got the chance to meet him. It was his first visit to Jerusalem and he could not stop asking questions about the Lord and the things he said and did. Luke told us that he wanted to write a "Life of Jesus" for circulation in the Gentile world where he was from.

Anyway, Paul had only been with us for about a week when a crowd of angry people grabbed him and loudly accused him of turning people away from the religion of the Fathers and of taking Greeks into the temple and defiling it. They started beating Paul right there in the street. The soldiers heard the shouting and sent a company to break up the crowd and arrest their victim. They put chains on Paul's wrists and ankles and arrested him without even finding out who he was.

Paul was held in confinement for two years in Jerusalem and Caesarea before he was taken to Rome, just as Peter had been.

Interviewer: James, what would you say is the most important thing you could say to the church today?

James: I would say that my brother, Jesus, did not live to share the love of God with a few chosen people, but to the whole world. When we think about the "whole world," we can't begin to know what all the people of the world are like. We can't understand how all the people of the world think or dream or love. But we know that because God loved the whole world, he sent his Son Jesus to tell the whole world of that love. And we know that before leaving us, Jesus said he wants us to go into the whole world and make believers and disciples of all the peoples of the world. So if there is anyone that God doesn't want included in the church, he didn't tell us. God wants everyone in the church, which is the family of his love. Everyone!

Interviewer: And finally, can you tell us what happened to you?

James: As I said, my ministry was in Jerusalem. I became known as the first bishop of Jerusalem. I was able to maintain a good reputation even among the Jews and Romans. Later I was known as "James, the Just" or "James the Righteous."

Finally, the Pharisees came to me and asked for my help in quieting the voices of the church who, they said, were continuing to disturb the people. They took me to the highest point of the temple and told me to shout out for the followers of Jesus to stop teaching in his name. When I refused, they pushed me off.

Interviewer: Oh no! How awful!

James: I survived the fall long enough to rise to my knees and to pray to our heavenly Father to forgive them for not knowing what they were doing. Then I died.

May I tell you one other thing I remember Jesus saying?

Interviewer: Of course. Please.

James: When we were just kids, a couple of us (I won't say which ones) were so stubborn that when we blurted out something that we were convinced was true, and it was pointed out to us that what we thought was true was not actually true, we would not change our minds no matter how much evidence was presented to us. We absolutely dreaded the thought that we might be wrong and others would know it!

Jesus told us the story about a man with two sons. One son wanted to leave home and convinced his father that he would be careful if the father would just give him all the money he would get when the father died. The father agreed, but before the son took the money and left, the father sat him down and told him all that he hoped the son would remember to do – and not do!

The other son stayed home and helped the father manage the farm. He worked hard. He did whatever was asked of him. He obeyed all the rules.

Word got back to the father that the son who had left home had not done what he had been told was expected of him by the father. In fact, he had spent all the money his father had given him and had nothing to show for it. When the older brother heard about the waste his younger brother had made of his life, and that he was coming home, he went to the father and said, "Father, I am so glad that I have done everything just the way you wanted. I don't think you should let my brother back into your house because of the things he has done."

But when the younger brother came up the path, the father went out and greeted him with open arms and brought him into the house and celebrated his return. The older brother stayed outside. The father went out and pleaded with him to come in and join the party. The older brother said, "Father, my brother has not lived the way you would have wished. He has done things that you have expressly forbidden us from doing. How can you possibly be comfortable having a person like that in your house?"

The father said to the faithful son, "No, I don't agree with the lifestyle your brother has lived or all the decisions he has made. But he is still my child and I want him in my family. And I want you to just love him and not judge him."

You see, both brothers had to admit that they had been wrong – the youngest had to admit that he wasn't capable of living without the guidance of his father, while the elder son had to admit that he would never be happy as long as he hated his brother.

My hope is that people of all times, especially those who are part of the church of Jesus Christ, will learn that there is no true happiness until we are willing to let go of the resentments and hatreds that are in our hearts and replace them with the love of Jesus. It is better to just love others rather than to try to be God's judges by condemning those people we think are wrong.

Interviewer: Thank you, James, for your leadership of the church in those terribly difficult times, and thank you for speaking to us today.

Chapter 13

Luke, the doctor
Colossians 4:14

Interviewer: In our next interview we will be talking to someone who never actually met Jesus face-to-face. This guest's name only appears three times in the New Testament, but he can tell us more about St. Paul than anyone else. Today's guest wrote just two books, but those books comprise more than twenty-five percent of the New Testament. His first volume lays out the work of Jesus Christ on earth in an "ordered account" (his words.) His second volume tracks the labors of the disciples and apostles in giving birth to the Church of Jesus Christ. Our guest travelled with Paul throughout Greece, Asia, Syria and Italy. Though he was from the western reaches of Asia, or Turkey as we know it, he did actually have the opportunity to visit Judea and Jerusalem with Paul. Our guest today is Dr. Luke.

Luke: It is a privilege to be with you today.

Interviewer: Before we get into your experiences with Paul, can you tell us a little about where you are from and how you came to be a doctor?

Luke: Certainly. I grew up in the region around the city of Pergamum which is between Mysia and Smyrna, north of Ephesus.

Pergamum was a prosperous city complete with temples, gymnasiums, aqueducts, and a theater that could seat 10,000 spectators. We also had a library that was considered second only to the Library of Alexandria in Egypt. Pergamum was one of the centers of healing focused on the god Asclepius. You might not recognize that name, but you have seen the staff of Asclepius on the medical symbols in your doctor's offices. It's the one with the snake wrapped around a staff. The venom of snakes was considered to have healing properties.

The Asclepian sanctuary with a large statue of the demigod drew thousands of visitors with various ailments yearly. As a boy, I was fascinated by the various "cures" the physicians there tried out. When I was old enough to get a job, I worked in the infirmary sweeping floors, changing and washing the linens and such odd jobs. I learned as much as I could by observing the techniques of the older physicians.

I did become a doctor in a few years, but let me dispel any thought you might have that doctors were healers. The most we could do for patients of our day was to ease their pain. Most of the things that made people sick were happening on the inside of their bodies and were, therefore, beyond our understanding. If they were going to live, they got better. If death was their fate, there was not much we could do to prevent it, though we were pretty good at setting broken bones and bandaging open wounds.

Interviewer: I'm sure you could entertain us all day with stories of your days as an active doctor. However, we really want to hear about your time with Paul. How did you meet? What was he like?

Luke: By my twenties, I had earned a place in the Asclepian circle of doctors. My experiences working there led me to understand that whether sick or not, most people were also carrying burdens of guilt or shame that were bearing down on them and just wearing them out. My mother was Jewish but my father was a Greek businessman. My mother had always told me the stories of her faith. Stories about the power of her God and his faithfulness to the Jewish people through the generations. I most liked the stories from Isaiah about the prophet who stood up and said,

> "Comfort, comfort my people! Says your God. Speak compassionately to [my people] and proclaim to [them] that [their] [pain] has ended, that [their] penalty has been paid, that [they] have received from the Lord's hand double for all [their] sins!
>
> Those who hope in the Lord will renew their strength; they will fly up on wings like eagles,

they will run and not be tired; they will walk and
not be weary." (Isaiah 40:1-2; 31)

You see, it was obvious that what we were doing as
physicians was perhaps helping, but in no way were we
healing.

By and by, we heard about a man who was spreading
the news about a rabbi who was a <u>true</u> healer. A rabbi who
could cast out the evil spirits of confusion and violence
that had hold of so many. A rabbi who could restore sight
and hearing and crippled limbs to strength. A rabbi who
forgave everyone, even those who nailed him to a cross.
That forgiveness brought peace to troubled hearts. The
man who was telling these stories about the rabbi named
Jesus was Paul. He said the one he spoke of was the one
that God had promised to send.

I had been too busy to pay much attention to stories
about Paul, until one day some of his friends came to the
Asclepian seeking help for their master. Since I was the
youngest physician on duty that day, my superiors sent me
to go and try to help the man. When I reached Paul, he
was doubled over in pain, unable to stand or walk.

I was told that he had been thrown from a horse a few
years back and had struggled with searing pain from time-
to-time ever since. I prepared a poultice of hot herbs and
spices and laid it across the small of his back. I told him
to stay down and try not to move. I said that if he felt no
relief by the morning to send for me again and I would
bring something stronger for him to take.

Sure enough, his men were back in the morning begging for me to return to him. I gathered some supplies and followed them back to Paul. But what greeted me was not a man in continuous pain, but a man standing and moving about with no limitation. When he saw me, he ran up to me and gave me a big hug and could not stop thanking me. I told him I was happy that what I had done had helped his pain.

The next thing he said took me by surprise. He invited me to stay with him and be ready to treat him again when his pain flared up the next time. He said he had plans to travel to Rome and eventually to Spain. Since the only pay I was getting at the clinic was a free meal each day and a place on the floor to sleep, it wasn't a difficult choice. At least with Paul I would have a chance to travel and see new places. So I said yes.

Paul stayed in the region of Mysia for several days. I had the opportunity to listen to Paul tell about the one he called his Lord, Jesus of Nazareth. He taught that this Jesus did nothing but talk about how God loves all people, yes, even Romans, and how God wants us to love everyone. He said that Jesus was sent from the God above to show us how to live lives of neighborliness and friendship, and he showed how to do that by sharing his healing power with everyone – even the Romans.

Paul told how, when the authorities got irritated at Jesus, he just kept healing the infirm and telling people that God has forgiven us of all our sins and tried to reach out to his accusers. When I got the chance, I asked

Paul just how it was that Jesus had healed people. What techniques did he employ?

Paul said that Jesus really did nothing spectacular. Mostly, he held their hands and prayed with them and encouraged them to go and live righteous lives. He said his methods were simple but the results were unbelievable!

People who had been crippled all their lives suddenly stood up and danced around. People blind from birth had their eyes opened and they could see for the first time. The deaf could hear after Jesus touched them. And those with obvious signs of leprosy were made clean by his touch.

"He touched lepers?" I exclaimed.

"I'm told that he did," Paul responded.

But the thing Paul talked about more than anything else was that Jesus had been executed by crucifixion, he was buried, but three days later he was alive again!

"You mean he literally rose up from death to live again?" I asked.

"That's right," said Paul, "but he didn't come back to seek retribution against those who had opposed him. He continued to announce that our God, who had sent him and in whose name he spoke, had forgiven every sin we could have committed. He said that he was entrusting to those who believe in him the same power over sin and death."

Paul told me that he had always prided himself on the power he had over those who disagreed with the law. He had the power to arrest, confine, interrogate, and execute those who defied the commands of the king. He said that at first all he knew about Jesus was that he led the people away from strict adherence to the laws of the king and the requirements of the temple priests, and that meant a loss of revenue at the temple.

He said he had been on a rampage to shut down the "Jesus movement" when he encountered Jesus himself on the road to the city of Damascus. He said he saw a bright light and was thrown from his horse. It was that fall that began his back pain, he said. He said that Jesus told him to go into the city and wait to be told what to do next. He said that what happened next did more to convince him of the truth of what was happening than any vision could.

Apparently the bright light had left him blind, so he relied on his companions to get him settled in a room in Damascus. It wasn't long before there was a knock on the door. His host, a believer named Judas, brought a guest into his room and introduced him as a Christian named Ananias.

"I was frightened," said Paul. "I mean there I was in the home of one of the people I had been sent to arrest. I was blind and defenseless. I assumed this Ananias was probably there to do me harm. Instead, he told me that his Lord, Jesus, had sent him to me to restore my sight. He said that he was afraid of me because he knew the purpose of my being there. But Ananias said that Jesus had told him that I had been chosen to carry his name before Gentiles, kings and Israelites."

Interviewer: Those had to be tense moments for both Paul and Ananias? What did Paul tell you happened after that?

Luke: Paul said that when the man touched his eyes, he could see again. He said Ananias invited him to be baptized. Paul said he had heard of baptism but was not clear on what it meant for Christians. Ananias explained to him that it meant two things. First, that the person receiving baptism was claiming Jesus as his Lord and Savior and rejecting the worldly forces of evil. Second, it was a sign to show how the forgiving, redeeming love of God was poured out over the baptized. With that explanation, Paul said that he gladly received the water and the Spirit of God.

Paul said that he stayed with the disciples in Damascus for several days while he grew stronger. He spent his time rereading the prophets and in the local synagogue in discussion with the elders. He said that he was convinced that Jesus was God's son, the Chosen One sent by God. The elders asked him how he knew that since he had been so dedicated against the message of Jesus.

Paul quoted the scriptures to them. He said that Jesus fit the description of the suffering servant outlined in Isaiah:

> He grew up like a young plant before us, like a root from dry ground. He possessed no splendid form for us to see, no desirable appearance. He was despised and avoided by others; a man who suffered, who knew sickness well. Like someone from whom people hid their faces, he was despised, and we didn't think about him. It was certainly our sickness that he carried and our sufferings

that he bore, but we thought him afflicted, struck down by God and tormented. He was pierced because of our rebellions and crushed because of our crimes. He bore the punishment that made us whole; by his wounds we are healed...but the LORD let fall on him all our crimes. He was oppressed and tormented, but didn't open his mouth. Like a lamb being brought to slaughter, like a ewe silent before her shearers, he didn't open his mouth. (Isaiah 53:2-7)

He said that from all he had heard, Jesus was kind to the poor and taught that we should be as well. He spoke to and prayed with Samaritans, lepers, Romans, Gentiles of all sorts. He never judged. He always encouraged. He walked with tax collectors and ate with sinners.

Paul said that he had always been impressed by power and that his goal was to be the most powerful person he could be. When he was given the power to put people to death, he thought he had made it "to the top." But upon learning that Jesus had the power to bring people to life and to give them a life that cannot be taken away, he realized that what he had thought was power was so common anyone could have it.

I had the opportunity to introduce Paul to my family and friends in Pergamum and soon a cluster of them began to meet for prayer in the name of Jesus.

Finally we moved on to Troas and by boat, across to Neapolis and Philippi. Philippi was named after Philip of Macedonia, father of Alexander the Great. Early in its history, gold was discovered in the hills and caves around the city making it a wealthy town with wealthy citizens. There are numerous springs bubbling up in the hills and along the Krenides River that runs alongside the city.

Finding no synagogue in the city, and it being the Sabbath, we went out to the river where we were told was a place of prayer for the Jews. We found a small group of women gathered at the river's edge. One woman who seemed to be something of a leader introduced herself to us as Lydia. Lydia told us they were "God worshipers", or Gentiles who had come to learn about and worship the God of Abraham.

After hearing Paul talk about Jesus, Lydia and others became excited by what they were hearing and wanted to hear more. After they were all baptized, Lydia invited the whole group of us to stay at her house. We wondered if she would have room until she told us that her profession was that of a dealer in purple. If you don't know, it was by imperial decree, that only citizens of a certain exalted rank could wear purple garments, it being such a sign of great wealth! Her clients must have all been loaded!

Daily, we went to the river to pray and teach, and daily the numbers of people who joined us grew. Along the way one day a slave woman, who was not in her right mind, attached herself to us. She was being used by her captors as a fortune teller in the marketplace and was apparently bringing in loads of cash for her handlers. She would tag along shouting, "These people are servants of God. They are proclaiming a way of salvation for you!"

What she was saying was not wrong, but after a few days, Paul decided that she was only doing it to create a commotion and draw attention to herself. So he stopped and addressed the spirit of confusion that seemed to be occupying her mind and said, "In the name of Jesus Christ, I command you to leave her!" And it did! In that very moment she became calm and attentive.

The men who owned her saw the change that came over her and realized that her ability to make them great amounts of money was suddenly dried up. They went straight to the police and accused Paul and Silas of interfering with commerce in the city. Paul and Silas were arrested, whipped and thrown in jail with their feet in stocks.

Rather than spending their time behind bars plotting an escape, Paul and Silas began singing hymns of faith and talking to the other prisoners about the Lord, Jesus Christ. About midnight there was an earthquake and the jail shook violently. The foundations of the jail shook and all the doors flew open.

When the jailer realized what happened and assumed the prisoners had all escaped, he knew he would be blamed so he raised his sword and was preparing to kill himself when he heard a voice calling from the dust cloud that filled the jail. "Don't harm yourself. We are all here!" was what he heard. When he was able to get a torch for light, he led them all outside where he was amazed to see each and every prisoner was still there.

The jailer asked Paul, "What must I do to be rescued?" Paul replied, "Believe in the Lord Jesus, and you will be saved – you and your entire household." Then the two of them, Paul and Silas, told him who the Lord Jesus Christ was and what he offered all of us. The jailer became so excited that he took Paul and Silas to his own home where he washed their wounds and sat them at his table. He gathered his whole household to listen to more stories about Jesus, and eventually, while it was still dark, they brought water and Paul baptized them all, even the children.

In the morning the authorities ordered that the prisoners all be released, since the jail was in too bad a shape to securely hold them. The jailer relayed this news to Paul and said they had been released and could go. But Paul wasn't about to leave until he made a point about what he saw as an abuse of the royal legal system. Paul found a policeman and said to him, "We are Roman citizens, but your bosses had us beaten publically without first giving us a hearing. They threw us into prison and now they want us to go away! No way! Those in charge need to come and escort us out of town lest the people think we are guilty of something.

When the "brass" heard this report, they could not get to Paul and Silas quickly enough, for the mistreatment of a citizen's rights could have ended in a death sentence for themselves. They brought gifts and apologized endlessly and begged them to leave the city peacefully.

Paul and Silas didn't leave Philippi immediately. They first went to Lydia's house where they encouraged the brothers and sisters to take care of each other. We also decided that I would stay behind in Philippi to shepherd the small group of believers which now included a rich family, a poor jailer and his family, and a few other women.

Interviewer: But you were a new Christian yourself who had never met Jesus. Weren't you afraid of that responsibility? What did you say?

Luke: You are exactly right. But I had been making notes along the way. As Paul and the others taught about the things Jesus did, I furiously wrote them down!

We did a lot of praying – a lot! We prayed for each other, for our families, for the disciples in Jerusalem which was under heavy discipline by the forces of Trajan. We prayed for guidance and forgiveness. In addition to praying, I shared the few stories that Paul had related to me about his life before and after he encountered Christ on that road.

Before he left, Paul wrote down a list for me -- a list of the ways he thought followers of the Christ should and should not live. We spent a lot of time reviewing that list and checking to see if we were living up to it.

Interviewer: I think I can guess, but could you tell us some of the things Paul listed for Christians to do?

Luke: He said that the message from the one we worshipped and followed was to make the world different by living differently from the way the world teaches.

Here, I have it right here. Let me read it to you: "Put to death the parts of your life that belong to the earth, such as sexual immorality, moral corruption, lust, evil desire, and greed." You see, when we are living that way, other people are more likely to be afraid of us than to want to be our friends. Those are the ways of living that make loving relationships hard to form.

He also said to set aside things like anger, rage, malice, slander and obscene language, and don't lie to each other.

Then he gave us a list of the things we should always try to do, ways we should try to live. "Be compassionate, kind, humble, gentle, and patient. Be tolerant and forgiving. And over all these things put on love, which is the perfect bond of unity."

I must say that I enjoyed the time I spent in Philippi. It is a beautiful city next to two refreshing rivers with plenty of fresh water flowing out of the mountains.

Interviewer: How long did you spend in Philippi?

Luke: It was about three years when I got a letter from Paul that he was going to come through Philippi on his way to Jerusalem and wanted to know if I would accompany him. Of course I said yes.

And so we made our way to Jerusalem. At each stop along the way, Paul reconnected with the small churches that had sprung up after his first visits with them. Those were loving and tearful goodbyes as Paul seemed aware that if he were going to make it to Rome and Spain, he wouldn't have the time to come that way again.

When we reached Caesarea, we went to the home of Philip the evangelist where we lodged for several days. Philip, along with his four daughters, had a lively congregation meeting in his home. One day, a man claiming to have prophetic powers came to the home and told Paul that it would be a tragic mistake for him to go to Jerusalem. He said they would bind his feet and turn him over to the Gentiles. When we heard this, we all tried to get Paul just to send a note to the church leaders in Jerusalem and invite them to come to Caesarea to meet with him.

Paul replied saying that he was not only prepared to be arrested in Jerusalem, but to die there as well for the sake of the name of Jesus.

It turns out that Paul was arrested and held in custody in Jerusalem and then Caesarea for more than two years awaiting some decision from the Romans. At least he could receive friends and guests. During those years, he continued to keep up correspondence with all the churches he had organized and the wonderful church leaders in so many places.

Interviewer: Did you stay with Paul in that time, and if you did, what did you do?

Luke: I did stay. In fact, I eventually accompanied him all the way to Rome where he spent his final years in jail awaiting a hearing before the emperor.

What I did during that time was to search out as many of the first disciples and others who had actually known Jesus and listen to their stories so I could organize them into an orderly account of his life and his impact on the world. I knew the day would come when those eye-witnesses would no longer be with us to tell their stories.

The most amazing moment, for me during that time was the day I was privileged to meet Mary, the mother of our Lord! She was making preparations to leave with John for Ephesus where he was building a small church and planning to stay and superintend that region.

I told Mary that I was preparing to write a book about the life of her son. I asked her what she could tell me that not a lot of people had already asked her about. She immediately asked if I wanted to hear about the night he was born. Not expecting that to be much of a story, I nevertheless said I would be happy to hear her tell it.

You know the story she told me about that most holy of nights and about the shepherds that visited. But what my words in retelling it never could relate was the tender emotion that was in her voice and the sweet expression on her face as she told it. It made me feel like I was in the presence of an angel and not just hearing about the angels that sang that night.

I think the thing that she cherished the most about that night was that our God and Father, the Creator and Master of all creation, had sent a whole host of heaven's angels to sing, not to some king, or some high priest, or rich businessperson, but to a group of shepherds. Shepherds were nobodies to most people. Shepherds were poor and dirty and often criminals. But they were the ones that our God chose to receive such a regal announcement!

When she finished telling me the story of his birth,

she asked me to be sure that in my book I told the whole world that God's love excludes no one! That all are loved!

Thank you for listening.

Interviewer: What a blessing it has been to hear your story. Thank you, Dr. Luke.

Chapter 14

Peter, the rock
John 21, Acts 2

Interviewer: Today we have invited Simon Peter back to talk to us about two events that occurred after Jesus' resurrection. Welcome back, Peter.

Peter: Good morning. It's good to be with you again.

Interviewer: Peter, the last time you were with us, you briefly mentioned that day after the resurrection when you had gone to the Sea of Galilee. You said that you and the others saw Jesus standing on the shore after you had fished all night and caught nothing. We would like for you to return to that moment and expand your telling of it. Would you do that for us?

Peter: Most certainly. As you may have surmised, that was, perhaps, the most pivotal moment in my life.

I had been to the empty tomb and we had all seen Jesus in the upper room in the days after he had risen. We had been together for several days when he said that he wanted to visit his friends and family in Capernaum while he was still with us. He instructed us to meet him in Galilee. I must tell you those days were all so confusing. We were having a hard time understanding what was happening. What did it all mean? What were we to do? We were still trying to absorb the fact that one who was dead was alive again. But what should we do? Where should we go?

So when he said, "Meet me at the lake," we left as soon as we could. Seven of us went, all the while wondering why we couldn't have travelled with him. When we got there, people had already seen Jesus. He got there a few days ahead of us and had been teaching the people and healing those who were sick. We didn't find Jesus right away, so we went to check on our boats. We decided to spend the night out on the lake and enjoy the cool breeze.

We had our nets out all night, bringing them in only a couple of times, but what we found in the nets was just trash - there weren't any fish. Our hearts weren't really into the fishing. We mostly just watched the stars and slept a little. Early in the morning, we heard a voice calling from the shore. Through the mist we could make out a man standing there, alone. He was calling to us, asking the question people always ask when they see someone fishing, "Have you caught anything?" I shouted back, "No." Then the man on the beach called out, "Try throwing your nets over the other side of the boat and you should have better luck."

That was a ridiculous suggestion. If there are no fish

on one side of the boat there won't be any on the other side. But we were all awake by then so we threw out the nets on the starboard side of the boat. Almost immediately the water was churning with hundreds of fish! We began to haul the net back into the boat but there were too many fish in it so we just tied it up to the side. While we were doing that, John said, "Peter, I think that is Jesus calling to us." I looked again and I could tell that he was right. Grabbing a garment, I dove in and swam to the shore. When I reached the beach and confirmed that it was indeed the Lord, I dropped to my knees and asked him to forgive me for all the doubts that still troubled me.

The others brought the boat to the dock, dragging the net full of fish. Jesus had already built a fire on the beach and had some bread cooking. He said, "Someone go and get some of the fish you have caught and let's have breakfast." I jumped up before any of the others and ran to the boat. I tried to pull the net from the water by myself, but there were too many fish in it, so I just grabbed an armful. (Later, one of the brothers counted more than a hundred and fifty fish in that net.)

As we sat there eating, we were all thinking the same thing, "Is this really Jesus? How did he get here so quickly?" But no one was brave enough to ask. However, by the way Jesus took the bread off the fire and divided it among us and the words he spoke as he gave us each a piece of fish to eat, we knew it was him. We could tell by the kind way he looked at each one of us as he handed us the fish. After that we sat and talked and joked and relaxed.

While the others rested and cleaned up a little, Jesus said quietly to me, "Simon, walk with me." We walked along the shoreline and soon Jesus asked me a question. He didn't look up, he just said, "Simon, do you love me more than these?"

I wasn't prepared for that! What did he mean, "More than these?" More than the fish we had just eaten? Those fish represented my livelihood. They fed my family. They were my security. Surely that was not what he was asking.

Was he asking if I loved him more than the other six disciples sitting by the fire loved him? More than Thomas, whom some said looked so much like Jesus that he could be his twin? More than Nathanael? More than James and John? More than all the others who had been together with him for three years and had been his students along with me? Or, was he asking if I loved him more than I loved the others. It was unlike him to stand us up against each other like that. Was this a test, I thought?

I knew the answer to the first part of the question, so I decided just to answer that. "Yes, Lord, you know I love you."

When I said that, Jesus said, again without looking up, "Take care of my lambs." Jesus always called the children "his lambs" and he always took time with the children. He always let them know that they were special to him, and he always made it clear to the grown-ups that the children were special to the Father and should never be ignored or exploited for labor or abused in any way. I thought to myself, yes, I can do that.

In a few moments, as we continued our walk, Jesus

turned to look at me and asked again, "Simon, do you love me?" I wondered what it must have been in my character that caused him to be so unsure of my devotion to him. What had I done to raise suspicion in him as to my loyalty and love for him? I had dropped the nets and left the boats when he called me to follow him, hadn't I? I had walked with him through the hills and mountains and along the desert roads. I had been his security when he was threatened. I had helped keep the others' arguments from getting to out of hand. I had been the first to openly declare that I believed he was the One sent by God to be our Savior. What more could I have done?

"Yes Lord, you know that I love you," I replied.

"I need you to take care of my sheep," Jesus said.

Taking care of sheep is not as easy as it looks, I thought. Sheep require constant attention to stay safe and healthy. Being a shepherd was not a job that brought great wealth or prestige. In fact, being a shepherd was generally a lowly position that drew scorn from more refined people. Shepherds were unwashed, uneducated, ill-bred, underpaid for the dangers they faced, and unwelcomed in the presence of important people. Jesus was asking me to be a shepherd to his people. Why would he ask me to do that?

Then I remembered the day he had said, "I am the good shepherd." He said the good shepherd lays down his life for his sheep. Was he asking me to be willing to lay down my life for the people he loved? Could I do that? I was all too painfully aware that I had denied knowing him the night of his arrest. I had denied it for fear that they would do to me what they were planning to do to hm. Now he was asking me if I could do that very thing. Could I lay down my life for his sheep?

A third time, as we walked, Jesus stopped and looked into my eyes. He asked, with an intensity in his voice that I had not noticed before, "Simon, son of John, do you love me?"

I was sad that he felt that he had to keep asking me if I loved him. I was thinking that maybe I had been a disappointment to him. I wondered if he was testing to see if I was up to some great mission he wanted to send one of us on. Was I smart enough? Was I strong enough? Would I be loyal enough? As I had those thoughts, I began to get excited thinking that he had selected me to head up the next great cause he was planning.

I suppose I swelled up with some pride when I answered, "Yes, Lord. You know everything. You know that I love you!"

"Then feed my sheep," he replied.

"Wait a minute," I thought. "That's it? That's all you think I can handle? That's how unimportant I am to you – just someone to feed your sheep?"

I was disappointed, and almost angry. But, as we walked, I remembered the day when we were right about at that same spot on the beach when Jesus told us that the crowd was following him just because they wanted more bread for their bellies; but that kind of bread would only feed them for a minute. He reminded them that it wasn't Moses who gave them the bread in the desert, it was the Father. He said, "The bread of God is the one who comes down from heaven and gives life to the world," and whoever eats of that bread of life will never be hungry again.

He was talking about himself. He was the one who came to feed people. He was the one who was giving life through his love and forgiveness. I began to think that was what this whole conversation had been about. He was telling me not just to pass out bread to the people, but to give them life by sharing the message he had shared with us, the message that the love we give to others is what will draw us close to the Father. The words of life are the food that his people really need!

Jesus was asking if I could feed the hearts of people with the words of life by the way I would live and the words I would speak. I had to ask myself, "Could I?" I finally said, "Yes," and he said, "Follow me." I'm sure Jesus is asking you the same questions. Can you answer, "Yes?"

Interviewer: Those are certainly questions we all should hear Jesus asking us, and we need to answer them over and over again throughout our lives.

Before we finish, please say a little more about the day the Holy Spirit blew over the church and brought it to life?

Peter: You know that a lot of training and conditioning goes into preparing for a big race, and then comes the moment when the starter's gun goes off and the race actually begins. Well, that Pentecost was like the firing of the starter's gun!

After we all returned to Jerusalem from the lake, we

were led by Jesus to the summit of the Mt. of Olives. While we were praying, an amazing thing happened. Jesus stood up and held his hands out over our heads and blessed us. As that was happening, he began to fade from our sight. It was as though he was being lifted up into the clouds. We all just stood there, still and silent. Suddenly there were two men in white standing with us. They asked us why we were just standing there gazing into the sky. They assured us that Jesus would come again in the same way we had just seen him go. With confusion and excitement mingled in our minds, we returned to the upper room in the house where we had been staying.

Not quite sure what to do, I suggested that we should elect someone to fill the empty spot left by Judas. After some discussion, Matthias was chosen and we all prayed.

We had all trained at the feet of the Master. We had been conditioning ourselves in fasting and prayer. We were like a team in that upper room just waiting for the signal! And boy did we get a signal!

Suddenly the wind literally blew the shutters off the windows! The room lit up with what I can only describe as tongues of fire above the head of everyone there, all one hundred and twenty or so of us. No one was burned, but we all began to shout our praises to God, only we weren't speaking our own language. We were speaking the languages of the many pilgrims who were in the city for the holiday.

With the windows open, the people on the street could hear our shouts and songs of praise. As they listened and tried to figure out what all the commotion was, some shouted up suggesting that we were all drunk! I was able to get to a window and waved my arms to get the crowd's attention. I shouted to them that we were not drunk. That it was only 9:00 in the morning after all! Then I reminded them of the words spoken by the prophet Joel:

> In the last days, God says, I will pour
> out my Spirit on all people.
> Your sons and daughters will prophesy.
> Your young people will see visions.
> Your elders will dream dreams.
> Even upon my servants, both men and
> women, I will pour out my Spirit
> and they will prophesy.
> I will cause wonders to occur in the heavens
> above and signs on the earth below,
> blood and fire and a cloud of smoke.
> The sun will be changed into darkness, and
> the moon will be changed into blood,
> before the great and spectacular day of the Lord comes.
> And everyone who calls on the name
> of the Lord will be saved.

(Acts 2:17-21)

"Fellow Israelites," I said, "listen to these words! Jesus the Nazarene was a man whose credentials God proved to you through miracles, wonders, and signs, which God performed through him among you. Many of you saw these things when he did them. In accordance with God's established plan and foreknowledge, he was betrayed.

You, with the help of wicked men, you had Jesus killed by nailing him to a cross. But God has raised him up! God has freed him from death's dreadful grip. It was impossible for death to hang on to him."

I went on to remind them that even our great king David talked about him. David said that he "saw that the Lord was always with him" and he "would not be shaken." David said that he would live in hope because the Lord promised not to abandon him in the grave, nor to permit his body to experience decay.

Then I told them that David died and was buried and his tomb was still there in that day, just down the road – they could go visit it! But Jesus, whom they murdered and buried, God raised up! We all saw him. Not only that, but we saw him taken up into heaven on a cloud where he sits exalted at the right hand of the Father. And now, we have received from the Father the promised Holy Spirit.

"What you are seeing today," I said, "is the result of the pouring out of that Spirit on us. Therefore, let all Israel know beyond question that God has made this Jesus, whom you crucified, both Lord and Christ."

Upon hearing this, they were deeply troubled and asked, "What should we do?"

I told them they should change their hearts and their lives. I said, "Each of you must be baptized in the name of Jesus Christ for the forgiveness of your sins. Then you will receive the gift of the Holy Spirit." Those who accepted my message were baptized. God brought about three thousand people into the church on that day! Like I said, it was like a shot went off and the church was underway!

Those were heady days. The twelve of us (including Matthias) spent every morning and evening teaching small groups of believers. The women organized the food that was being donated and prepared the meals. A sense of awe came over the whole enterprise as people were quickly learning other languages from their new friends, taking care of the sick among whom God was performing many wonderful signs!

The believers who lived in Jerusalem were opening their homes to the ones who had come from out of town. Others, we learned, were selling pieces of property they had and were contributing some or all of the proceeds from those sales.

At three o'clock each day, we went to the temple for prayers. At first we went with some trepidation for fear of the authorities. But it was soon obvious that those authorities were more afraid of the crowds of people who were drawn to us than we were of them. We quickly learned that a good way to make friends is to talk about love and to feed the bodies and souls of those who are hungry. That's what we did, and it worked. So many people were wanting to be baptized and to join our movement that we never stopped to ask ourselves if Jesus would want this person or that person or that kind of person in his church. We just fed them and loved them and the church grew.

It wasn't long though before the devil worked his way into the hearts of some members. They began to question whether some people were worthy of being called one of Christ's. They said things like, "Those people don't wear the kind of clothes Jesus wore," or, "That group eats shellfish," or, "They do things we don't think Jesus would agree with," or, "They are not circumcised -- Jesus would never accept them."

I have to admit I struggled with those thoughts myself in the beginning. But the day came when I had a vision, and God set me straight. It was just before lunch and I was hungry. I was dozing off when I saw this large sail being lowered down from heaven. In that sail were all the kinds of animals that our Jewish people would never eat. I was repulsed until I heard a voice say, "Take something to eat, Peter." In response, I said, "No, Lord. I will not eat any of these unclean animals. It would be against your laws." But then the voice of God said clearly to me, "Peter, if I have called something clean, what right do you have to call it unclean?"

I knew that God wasn't talking to me about animals, but about people. What right do I have to consider any people or person that God has created unclean or unwelcome? How can we keep any person that God has created out of the fellowship of the church?

And then, just to make sure I got the point, I suppose, I was told to go to the home of a Gentile, Roman soldier, to preach the gospel and baptize the entire household. I got the point! God doesn't consider anyone unworthy or unwelcome in his church. The love of God excludes no one!

I know that is still a question that the church of Jesus Christ struggles with in your day. I know that there are some who figure certain others are not worthy enough to be let in, and that is sad. Let me just end by reminding you that our Lord said that he came to judge the world with righteousness, but that we are not to judge anyone. We are simply called to love, and teach, and heal, and forgive.

Will you pray with me?

> Father, we have no right to withhold the fellowship of your family from any child of yours. When you call us to be gatekeepers of your church, you are calling us to be there to welcome the world in, not to keep anyone out. Reassure us that your church on earth is mightier than any sin of any one person. Lead us into tomorrow with hearts intent on loving and not on judging; intent on building and not barricading. Through the power of your Holy Spirit, help us to be more like Jesus in all that we speak and do. In his name we pray and live. Amen.

Interviewer: Thank you, Peter, for that reminder and encouragement.

Peter: Before I go, I would like you to meet a young man with quite a story to tell.

Chapter 15

A Boy and his lunch
John 6:1-14, Matthew 5:1 - 7:29

Interviewer: What is your name young man?

Samuel: My name is Samuel.

Interviewer: Tell us, please, how it was that you came to know Jesus and his disciples?

Samuel: Well, I was much younger then, about ten or eleven years old. Jesus had been in the region on the north shore of the lake for several days and everyone was talking about him. One day I asked my father if I could go and listen to him. Father agreed and mother packed some food in a paper tied with a string and gave it to me. "In case you get hungry," she said.

It wasn't hard to find where Jesus was that day, I just followed the dust cloud created by the crowd that was following him. As we walked along, I tried my best to wiggle through the people to get close to Jesus. I got close, but before I could get to him, Jesus led us up on a hill and made everyone sit down. When I sat, I was only a few feet away from where Jesus was standing.

He really caught my attention with one of the first things he said: "Happy are people whose lives are harassed because they are righteous, because the kingdom of heaven is theirs. Happy are you when people insult you and harass you and speak all kinds of bad and false things about you, all because of me. Be full of joy and be glad, because you have a great reward in heaven. The people harassed the prophets who came before you in the same way." (Matthew 5:10-12)

I thought he was talking just to me. You see, at that time one of my legs was shorter than the other and my foot was twisted in such a way that it made me walk with a very noticeable limp, more of a skip, really. The other kids all made fun of me. Not only would they try to imitate the way I walked, they would throw things at me and call me all kinds of names. They would tell me that I was worthless and should just go and jump into the lake. I knew what it was to be harassed and insulted. He was talking to me and he was saying that I would be rewarded in heaven! I couldn't believe it. I just sat and listened to everything he said after that.

Interviewer: Can you tell us what else you remember Jesus saying that day?

Samuel: He said we were "the salt of the earth." We all knew what he meant. He meant that just like salt changes and preserves food, we would change the world! I didn't know how, at the time, but he said it with such strength that you had to believe him. Then he said we were to be lights for the world. He said that a city on a hill could be seen at night when the lamps were all lit, and that no one would light a lamp and then put a barrel over it. He said that the good things we did were our lights and we should let people see them so they would be encouraged to do the same kinds of things.

He talked about the ancient laws that we were all taught, but he said them a little differently. He said that when the law said, "Don't commit murder," that was a good thing. But, he said, we should not even get angry with people. He said that if we call someone a name like "idiot" or "fool" we will be punished because anger leads to worse things like fighting or injury and we might even be dragged into the court for saying those things.

He said that men and women should stay away from each other unless they are married. And he said that we young people should not even think about doing anything shameful to a girl because that is just as bad. And he told the grown-ups that if they are married they should stay married. He explained that women were helpless against the strength of a man and that a divorced woman would be left with nothing since her husband would keep everything they owned – even the children!

He talked about not making promises you couldn't keep and not trying to get even with someone who has hurt you. I remember exactly what he said. He said that if someone slaps or hits you on your cheek, rather than hitting them back you should just turn so they could hit you on your other cheek as well. That caused quite a stir among the men in the crowd. And when he added that if someone steals your shirt you should offer them your coat as well, I heard all kinds of voices saying, "No! You can't mean that!"

But when he said that we should love our enemies like we love our neighbors, I thought people might leave. But he reminded us that the God of heaven makes the sun rise and shine on evil people as well as good people. And that when the rain falls it waters the fields of our enemies as well as our own. People seemed to calm down a bit when he said that. He explained that if we only love the people who love us we are no different from the evil people who also love the other evil people who love them. He said that even tax collectors and Gentiles do the same thing. He taught us that our heavenly Father shows love to everyone and that if we want to do what God wants we need to love our enemies.

"But," he said, "Don't go around bragging about how good you are." He said don't go into the place of prayer and blow a trumpet to attract attention to your good deeds. He said that if you do, other people might be impressed, but God won't be. He said we should do good just to be helpful and not for the praise we might get from others.

Then he talked about praying. Again he said that we should not make a big show out of praying. He said that when we pray we should go off by ourselves and pray in secret. He said to go into our room and shut the door if necessary. "And don't worry," he said, "God will hear you."

He even taught us how we might pray. It was a beautiful prayer that goes something like this:

"Our Father who is in heaven,"
(He said that we should think of
God as our loving father.)
"Holy is your name"
(I think he was referring to the commandment
against taking God's name in vain.)
"Bring your kingdom to earth just like it is in heaven."
(Jesus had often talked about the kingdom
of God as a being kingdom of love.)
"Give us the bread we need for today."
(He was reminding us that just like the manna the
people ate in the wilderness, God would provide all
that we would need each day and that we should
not be greedy and try to collect more than we
need. We should trust God for our "bread."
"Forgive us for the ways we have sinned against you,
Just as we will forgive those who
have sinned against us."
(He was saying that as much as we want to be
forgiven, God wants us to be forgiving.)
"And lead us away from temptation to do wrong,
And rescue us from the evil we are tempted to do."
(Temptation and evil are all around us and it is so easy
to give in to the desire to do things that hurt. But if we
will follow God, God will lead us away from all that.)

He said we should not pray or fast just to be seen. God hears us and knows the good we do. He said we should not worry about getting rich. Thieves can steal our money but they cannot take away the goodness that awaits us in heaven. He said we should not worry about our lives, about what we are going to eat or about the clothes we wear. He said that God feeds the plants in the field – even the weeds, and God clothes them in beautiful colors – even the weeds. He said that we are much more important to God than any of the plants or animals. He said that not even King Solomon was dressed like the flowers in the field. "God knows that you need these things," he said. He said that all we need to do is look for God's kingdom of love and righteousness and work to be a part of that. God will take care of the rest.

Interviewer: Is there anything else you remember hearing Jesus say?

Samuel: Oh, there was so much more. He said that if we don't want other people constantly judging us, we should not judge others. He said that God knows how to give good things to us and we should only give good things to others. That if there is anything we want to know, we should just ask God about it.

He ended his teaching that day with a story about two men who built houses for themselves. He said that one man was in such a hurry that he didn't dig his foundation deep enough and just built his house on the sand. The other man took his time and dug down until he hit bedrock and built his house on a firm foundation. Both houses looked beautiful and strong when the men were finished, but the day came when there was a violent storm and the rain and winds blew against both houses. The house built on the bedrock weathered the storm with little damage, but the house built on the sand was washed away.

He didn't really have to, because I think we all got his point, but he finished by saying that those houses represent our lives. If we build our lives on falsehoods, or on greed, or on hatred, then they will not withstand the storms that will surely come.

Interviewer: Peter told us there is quite a story about what happened after Jesus finished preaching that day. Please tell us what happened next.

Samuel: It was late when he finished and we were all getting pretty hungry. Jesus suggested that his disciples go and find food to feed the crowd. One of them said to Jesus that there was no way that they had enough money to buy food for a crowd that big. While his disciples were standing there trying to figure out what to do, I was able to reach one of them and tug on his robe. He turned and asked me what I wanted. I held up the small package of food that I had with me and asked him to give it to Jesus because he looked like he was hungry as well.

He asked me what I had and I told him it was just a little bread and a couple of small fish that my mother had packed for me. That disciple, who I later found out was Peter's brother, Andrew, reached out his hand, I thought to take the package, but he took my hand and helped me to my feet and led me straight to Jesus. He told Jesus that I was offering him my own lunch.

Jesus first asked me what my name was, and when I told him it was Samuel he said, "Just like the old prophet that God called into his service." Then he asked me what I had in my lunch package. I told him it wasn't much but that I thought he looked hungry and I wanted him to have it. He thanked me and asked me to pray with him. He asked God to bless me and the food I had offered. He asked that everyone there would be able to share my little lunch. When he was through praying, he gave each of his twelve helpers a small piece of the bread and some fish and told them to go and feed the people.

I was confused. How could he think that such a small amount could possibly feed so many? Sitting there next to Jesus, I watched as the disciples moved from group to group holding out their hands for people to take something to eat. They kept going and going and they never ran out! When they were done and came back to Jesus, he gave each of them a basket and instructed them to go around again and collect anything that was left over.

At first they just stood there looking puzzled. But Jesus waved his hand at them and said, "Go." They went back around through the crowd and when they returned a second time their baskets were all filled with bread and fish! Jesus turned to me and said, "Remember, Samuel, God knows what you need and God will provide for you. And don't ever think that what you have to offer is not enough to make a difference. With the Father all things are possible."

I got up the nerve to ask Jesus about what he had said at the beginning of his teaching that I could be happy even when the other kids were harassing me and calling me names. Jesus said that he loved me and that I should always remember that the Father in heaven loves me and that long after those other kids were gone, God would still love me.

After that day I tried to always find something that I could do to help someone, and the more I did that, I realized that I wasn't being laughed at so much.

Interviewer: Wow! What a story Thank you for sharing it with us.

Printed in the United States
by Baker & Taylor Publisher Services